Reaching for the Sky

Reaching for the Sky

Writers of Kern Anthology 2018

WOK Press

ISBN-13: 978-0578411637

Design by Cynthia Bermudez
Layout by Dennis VanderWerff
Cover Image © Lori Lovelady

This anthology contains the work of members of Writers of Kern (WOK), a branch of the California Writers Club. The authors hold the copyrights to their work and retain full rights.

WOK Press is an imprint of Writers of Kern.

Writers of Kern
P.O. Box 22335
Bakersfield, CA 93390-2335
writersofkern.com

CONTENTS

POETRY

FALL CONTEST WINNERS

ACKNOWLEDGMENTS

A goal of Writers of Kern is to encourage its members to write for publication. *Reaching for the Sky* offers a path to achieving that goal.

Over the last eight months our editorial team took on a huge mission. We read, reread, and selected a variety of work submitted by WOK members. We took our tasks seriously, making sure the pieces you are about to read are a collection of WOK members' finest work.

To our dedicated editorial team, thank you for the time spent reading and editing the numerous submissions. I am grateful to Mandy Wallace for the inspirational cover design and to Cynthia Bermudez for expertise in design, formatting, and publishing.

To Dennis VanderWerff, thank you for being as passionate as I am about making our anthology dream a reality. Your encouragement and wisdom mean more than you know.

And to our members, I offer a heartfelt thank you. You braved the submission process and shared your treasured work. You made it possible to reach for the sky.

Joan Raymond
Bakersfield, California

EDITORS

Joan Raymond, *Senior Editor*

Editing Team

Annis Cassells
Clarissa Kae
Donnée Harris
Karen Sallee
Mandy Wallace
Shelley Evans

MUSEFUL MOMENTS

Museful Moments—a standard activity at Writers of Kern monthly meetings—are quick-write responses to one- or two-word prompts. Members and guests write for three minutes. Three or four responses are shared with the group.

CHANGE

Terry Redman

I'm weary of changes in my health, my life. My right eye has always seen poorly. My right needs glasses. Cataract surgery but the left eye that now has macro degeneration. The "good eye," is not so good, bad one is worse,

This week, today, I have (uh) seen a change for the worse on the right. Poor vision has gotten worse affecting actions large and small. Walls creep up and surprise me, items in the grocery store change as I reach for them. Damn this right eye.

Typing is trickier; my fingers miss the key confusing Word and reding tbt iPad is too hard. My time on the computer is down to 20 minutes.

The right eye pairs up with my right leg to make balance a challenge. Night driving is long over and a recent near accident scared me so much my wife does most driving.

PUMPKIN

Janet Skibinski

It was a crisp, sunny fall day. The leaves crunched like corn flakes beneath our feet. Andrew, Alex, and Ayden, our three grandsons, were going to their first Pumpkin Patch to select the perfect gourds that would become their jack o' lanterns.

Ayden was 14 months old and communicated with grunts, pointing, and jabber. As we walked up and down the rows of bright orange orbs, Ayden suddenly pointed to a giant round gourd.

"Pun kin!" He laughed gleefully. Everyone turned and smiled and said, "Did you hear that? His first word!"

Nelson Varon

His eyes lit up
Like distant triangles on an outer planet.
His smile was half mixed with a tinge of sadness
As he recalled memories of other pumpkins
Whose dancing eyes and crooked smiles lay crumbled
On over-ripened faces.

For a brief moment in time, however,
He delighted in knowing
That he alone provoked
The "ooohs" and "aaaahs" and "giggles"
Of countless children as they gazed upon his eerie
glances Piercing the darkness.

RAIN

Janet Skibinski

I remember that wet stuff called rain. I remember thunder and lightning so severe the windows in our century-old home rattled their protest. Occasionally, the water from the Mill Creek, located just a few blocks away, would be clogged with debris causing the backup to gush out of the drains in our basement. In the summer, we danced with our umbrellas in imitation of that famous dancing couple on film. Our flip-flops flipped and flopped off our feet and we squished through the grass of the lawn.

WASHING MACHINE

Nelson Varon

It was like clockwork. Every Sunday, the old Maytag in the kitchen, with its hand-rollers poised to squeeze the last drop of water from the rinsed clothing, would be laying on the floor without shame or embarrassment as all of its inner parts were exposed for all to see by the once-a-week mechanical surgeon of the house, my father.

When he reassembled the machine, which wasn't broken in the first place, it amazingly looked and worked no better than it had before.

PAPER

Janet Skibinski

Newspaper, note paper, colored paper, paper boats, party hats, napkins, placemats, tissues, toilet paper – where would we be without paper? We'd have nothing to wrap old fish in, write reminders on, do origami, sail on a lake, celebrate with, wipe your mouth on, blow your nose in, keep your table clean, write Museful Moments on, or keep the Charmin company going!

FEATHER

Nelson Varon

It skips freely, then floats calmly in the air.
Carried gently by currents of unseen breezes,
It is framed by the infinite blueness of the universe.

Suddenly, as though playing some whimsical game,
It erratically whips up to the left, then up to the right,
Then gleefully flutters as though proud of its acrobatic display.

Wait! Where did it go? Aha! It's playing hide and seek.
I see it now, perched high on the branch of a newly-blossomed tree,
Mingling secretly amongst the mint-green leaves of spring.

LIVER

Brent Gill

When I agreed to go to dinner at my girlfriend's house, the very last thing I expected to be served was raw liver. Jane told me her mom was a little unusual, but I did not anticipate a blood-red slab of liver quivering on my plate. Do I salt it? Do I cut it into tiny pieces? And what if I gag at the sight and taste of uncooked liver? When I looked aghast at it, they laughed out loud, Jane the loudest.

COMPUTER

Pam Reeves

Oppositional Defiance Disorder is just as terrifying as it sounds.

When I ask her to do something, she shuts down – it's as if I don't exist. When we are interacting, she stops everything and freezes, even closing her eyes, mocking me. When we go to the next shopping spot, she starts barking for everything she sees, squawking noises I've never heard before. Explosive outbursts pop up, making me crazy.

I put her on a time out last week. She went to the computer repair shop for a day. She's compliant… for now.

MEMOIR

THE GOLDEN PINE CONES

Brent Gill

"Brent, wake up. We have a firefighter to transport. Meet me at the Medical Tent."

During the summer I'm a contractor for the U.S. Forest Service. I drive my pickup on various assignments in support of the firefighters. On this occasion I was assigned to the Soberanes Fire, southeast of Carmel. The man summoning me was the Transportation Manager.

A firefighter using a chainsaw got a small chip of wood in his eye. I needed to take him to the Emergency Room, though it was already 10:00 p.m. He was examined and treated, then released to duty. Exhausted, I crawled back into bed at 3:30 a.m.

Because I had worked overtime, I was required to take ten hours "mitigation time" before returning to duty. By midmorning I was awake and restless so asked permission to leave the fire camp.

I remembered our 1965 honeymoon in Carmel, when my bride fell in love with a unique, one-of-a-kind piece of jewelry. As newlyweds, we couldn't possibly afford the solid gold pine cone pendant. However, on a return trip in the early 1980s, Sharon was finally able to buy her cone. Though in typical male fashion, I forgot about her purchase.

I had extra money and wanted to find something nice to take to her from Carmel. As I drove down Carmel Valley Drive, I pondered what to buy. I knew I wanted something shiny and sparkling.

I remembered seeing the tiny cones in several stores around Carmel. I was confident I could find one now. After examining displays in several locations, I hadn't found any cones.

I asked one store clerk if she knew where I could find this unique item. She'd never seen what I described. She suggested I ask the gentleman in the jewelry store around the corner. "He's been there forever. I bet he'll know where you can find them."

I turned the corner and tried the door. Though locked, the lights were on and the *Open* sign was in the window. I peered inside. The man behind the counter waved. I rattled the door and pointed to the sign. Instead of opening up, he walked to a side door.

"Yes sir? May I help you?"

I told him about our honeymoon in Carmel over half a century before. Now I wanted to find a special gift for my best girl. "Do you have any idea where I can find those magnificent golden pine cones she loved?"

I'll never forget the expression on his face. He grinned, apparently pleased. "I made them. My name is Kirkor Kocek. This is my jewelry store. Please come in." He led me into his workshop, locking the door behind us.

"You're lucky to find me here. Monday is my day off. Normally I'd be home, but I have some work to finish."

"I want to get a gift for my wife, but I can't find those beautiful pine cones anywhere."

"I haven't made any cones for nearly thirty years." He smiled broadly. "But I've been thinking about making them again."

With a twinkle in his eye, he said. "Let me show you something."

He pulled over a step-stool, climbed up and opened a high cupboard. Digging around in the back he pulled out a small box, then stepped down. Removing the top, he showed me a couple of dry twigs with tiny brown cones attached.

"I cast plaster around these. When the mold is dry, I burn out the cone material, then pour in the gold. This makes a perfect replica. Each cone is unique, for in nature, no two are alike."

I asked Kirk if he could create a necklace and pair of earrings I could afford. He assured me he could, but it would take a month for him to produce a finished product. Though disappointed, I agreed. I'd hoped to take them home with me.

Before returning to fire camp food, I enjoyed a great lunch along Ocean Boulevard and contemplated my surprise. I became excited about the prospect of us making a return trip to Carmel to pick up Sharon's gift. It would be a long month waiting for Mr. Kocek to finish his work.

Sometime after midnight, I woke with a start. Depressed, I remembered the little gold pine cone Sharon purchased long ago. For a few minutes the excitement of giving my wife a special gift evaporated.

Then I had an excellent idea. I could take the money I was planning to put into the necklace, and instead add small diamonds to the earrings. I knew Sharon would like anything with diamonds. Even tiny stones would make the earrings sparkle. Content now, I went back to sleep. The next morning I sent Kirk a note describing the change I wanted.

After working fourteen days, I needed to return home for two mandatory days off. While there, I poked around in my wife's jewelry boxes, trying to find the cone I believed she'd purchased years earlier. My search met with no success.

On the way back to fire camp, I called our youngest son. "Call your mom. Make up any story you like, but make sure she has one of the little gold cones. I want to be certain she knows where it is, so she can wear it with the earrings I'm getting her."

The next afternoon our son reported back. "She definitely has one of those gold cones. I told her I wanted to get something like it for my wife. She got it out so she could describe it to me. Don't worry, Dad. She doesn't have a clue."

Two days later, instead of the month he'd requested, I got a text from Kirk, complete with a picture. The earrings were nearly ready.

Apparently my story of the love for my wife, and wanting to give her something special, had appealed to him.

Friday was my last day of duty on the Soberanes Fire. I'd promised Sharon I would be home in time to go to her class reunion on Saturday. Late Friday afternoon I picked up the finished earrings. They were beautiful.

Saturday morning I began my journey home. As I drove, I thought with great pleasure how much my wife would enjoy wearing her gift.

Fifteen miles away from home I called Sharon. "Where are you, sweetheart? Are you getting ready to go to the reunion? I want to see you as soon as I get home. I have a big surprise."

She admitted later, she thought I'd picked up a little dog at the fire and wanted to show her our new pet to make sure it was all right.

My puzzled bride met me on the back patio. We sat down. I handed her the special bag from Kocek Jewelers.

"What's this?"

"Open it and see."

As she unwrapped the beautiful box, a look of comprehension crept across her face. "Does our youngest son know about this?"

I assured her he did. As fast as possible, she finished unwrapping her gift.

The gold pine cone earrings, accented with two tiny sparkling diamonds, were as big a hit as I'd hoped.

And, yes, we both cried.

VACANT EYES

Judy Kukuruza

"How could you be so stupid? What were you thinking?"

The mother grabbed the child's chin and yanked her small face around to make her look at her as she berated her. "Look at me!"

The child made an effort to look at the mother, but everything was blurry, distorted.

"I said, what were you thinking? Why do you do such thoughtless and stupid things? Look at me! LOOK AT ME! What is wrong with you? Answer me!"

The child shrugged her small shoulders and looked at the floor. Her silence may have been what the mother witnessed, but her head was full of thoughts, words, explanations that she knew would not be accepted.

"You just wait till your daddy gets home. You better come up with a good answer for him! I don't know for the life of me why you act like you do! You are my cross to bear! Now, get out! Go outside! GO!" and the mother turned the little girl away from her and pushed her forcefully toward the back screen door. The little girl obliged her by kicking open the door and shuffling out, letting it slam behind her. She heard, "What have I told you about kicking the door and letting it slam" yelled behind her. She smiled and headed on to her tree, where nothing and no one could reach her.

Feet hanging limply as she straddled a limb, she looked up to see what cloud shapes there might be, if there were any birds flying free… and she went inside herself. There was peace inside. Acceptance. She dozed.

The sound of her father's truck tires crunching on the gravel woke her and she sighed with a resignation that came from knowing that she would most likely get a whipping and go to bed hungry because bad girls did not eat supper. She watched him get out of the truck, slam the door behind him, enter the house and let the screen door slam behind him there, too. Well, she wouldn't yell at *him* for letting it bang shut. She wondered if she should voluntarily climb down to face her parents or wait to be called. She decided to wait it out. Maybe the mother would have forgotten whatever sin she had committed, or the father would be too tired to punish her for upsetting the mother. One could always hope. But then she heard her father yell for her to come inside and with another sigh she crawled out of the tree.

Punishment was swift and sure but this time, the closet was added. After a whipping and a promise of no supper without a contrite apology, which she knew she would never offer, she was to sit in the closet to think about her "sins" until she was told she could come out. When offered a chance to apologize immediately, she opted not to, and the closet door was shut and she sat in the dark, thinking—not about apologies she could offer, but rather about how she could get even. Often, her way of getting even consisted of spitting on the mother's dresses that hung around her head or in her shoes that littered the closet floor. But she was hot, tired, and out of spit so she tried to be more creative.

In her pondering, she let her hands feel the mother's dresses. It was too dark in the closet to see which dress was which, colors, or anything like that. But her fingers did find the lace on the bottom of one dress and she grinned, knowing it was her mother's favorite dress up dress. She poked one small finger through the lace and felt for any loose threads. Having plenty of time to explore in the dark, she pretended she was learning to read braille and kept poking her fingers through the lace. Finally, her fingers found a single thread. Her little mouth grinned widely as she tugged on the thread. At first it stubbornly would not pull free, but then, to her delight, she felt it unravel and become looser. She yanked a little and it loosened more. She became intent on the pulling of the thread and more of it came loose. She stifled a giggle and pulled more and more.

As the thread unraveled the lace, she began to hear plates being set on the table and knew the family would sit down to eat. She did not feel any hunger she was so intent on unraveling the lace from the bottom of the mother's favorite dress. She simply kept on pulling the now willing thread, enjoying her life immensely. Then suddenly, the closet door opened wide. Her eyes had to adjust to the sudden light and she saw her father's form standing there, telling her to get up and get out of the closet and go to bed. She struggled to get to her feet from her cramped position and realized she was covered in the thread she had pulled, and it was entangling her legs and feet. She laughed aloud and the mother, who had come into the room to see what was taking so long, shrieked as she saw what the child had done. It was a regular cacophony of conflicting shrieks, laughter, and yelling.

When the little girl had been whipped again and was in bed, she told her teddy bear of her great adventure in the closet and softly laughed to herself again. Little didn't mean stupid. And like her father always said, if you worked at something hard enough, you'd win. By golly, she had found the way because she sure had worked hard and won. That night, the little girl smiled her way into sleep. It hadn't been a bad day at all. It had been fun!

Her eyes became vacant. The smile stayed.

IT'S GETTING DARK BUT THERE ARE STARS

Julie Bonderov

In my early 20's, Mom told Dad, "You'd better enjoy it while you're doing it Jack, because you won't remember it later." He had a notoriously poor memory. Even when I was a teen, it was common for Dad to ask me something and then ask me the same thing shortly after. I assumed either he wasn't a good listener, or he was just distracted. Maybe it was Attention Deficit Disorder before we knew there was such a thing.

Dad was a hardworking, "do-it-yourself" man. Though he worked as a full-time pharmaceutical salesman, he built the fences around our home, landscaped the yard, put in the sprinklers and patios and built a fountain out of the extra cement. He designed and built his own aerodynamic, locking cartop luggage carrier for our cross-country vacation trips and painted it to match our car.

He'd buy Volkswagens with blown engines and rebuild them so that we had some very economical second vehicles. Dad used one of those, *Volkswagen Repair for the Complete Idiot* -type books. He gave me my own copy when I drove to college in one of those VWs.

I was his assistant in many of these tasks so I wasn't afraid to tackle similar chores myself as a single woman. Working with him was one way to spend time together.

My favorite project of his was when he saw a promotion by Kool cigarettes to earn a small, two-person sailboat by collecting the brand's proof-of-purchase tags. Dad didn't smoke so he asked all his friends and neighbors to switch to Kools so he could get the sailboat. They did, and we were the proud owners of a 12-foot styrofoam boat with a green and white sail that said "KOOL."

Of course, Dad improved the boat. He covered it with a coating of a fiberglass so the foam didn't get nicked and broken and painted it red. He lacquered the dagger board and tiller so they'd last forever too. We'd lower the boat from the garage rafters with the pulleys he'd devised, put it on the roof rack of the car and take it to Del Valle Reservoir on the roof of a VW. Two people could unload it from the car roof and spend a delightful day relaxing on the lake.

Dad is in his mid-eighties now and may ask the same question five times in a 15-minute conversation. He used to help me with many of my computer issues, but now needs help with his own computer. For many years Dad took care of his older sister's hearing aids when she no longer could. Now he gets confused changing his own batteries and may put the old ones back in and throw the new batteries away. I watch and grieve.

My mom is changing as she ages along with my dad.

She was a kindergarten teacher in the days before kindergarteners were supposed to be able to read. She said, "A child's experience in kindergarten can set the tone for their whole attitude about school." I remember going to her classroom as a child and enjoying playing with the toy kitchen and store, and dress-up things that are no longer a part of kindergarten.

Mom shared her love of reading and words with my brother and me. We grew up to be readers with good vocabularies and have passed these joys on to our children. I think she dreamed of being a journalist or reporter. My mom loved to write our Christmas letters as a yearly record of family events. When I asked my mom to write down a history of the events of my life, she did!

I had asked my mom to do this for me because I seemed to have inherited my dad's poor recall and one of Mom's roles was, "Family Memory Keeper." I was aware of sharing this weakness with my dad and once told him, "Dad, if something ever happens to Mom, we'll both lose our memory." And now it's happened.

I noticed Mom remembered some significant events differently than she had previously. She wasn't able to supply answers about the past like she used to. She completely forgot things that were said or done. Then she struggled to find words. (I am now graced with the "gift of interpretation." I often supply the word she's needing - even if she uses hand motions to express a hint.)

About a year ago, Mom said, "I used to be a good wife."

I said, "You're still a good wife. What do you mean?"

"I used to handle the bills and finances, but now I can't," Mom replied. I just hugged her.

Mom still takes the crossword puzzle out of the paper every day. But none of the boxes have letters in them anymore.

In the midst of this sorrow and loss, there are sparkles of grace, humor and sweetness. I take my parents for rides in the car and they really enjoy the view - it's all new to them! When the moon rose large and clear before it was even dark, my mom said, "Look at that moon! I've never seen anything like it!" Instead of saying, "I'm sure that sometime in your 86 years you have," I said, "It's amazing, isn't it?" and I paused and appreciated it with them.

We laugh together. I can repeat the same story and still get a laugh because they don't remember that I already told it. We even laugh about forgetting. One of the times they denied having any memory issues, I quipped, "Did you forget that you have memory problems?" More laughter.

One evening Mom and I were arguing. I knew better than to argue with someone with her condition, but still did. Dad did something he'd never done before. He walked in and took both of our hands and started praying out loud, "God, thank you that Julie's here. We need help now and Julie's here to help us." No more argument from either of us. Just tears and hugs.

In this time of diminishment, my parents still bless and encourage others.

When my aunt who lived in the same senior community died, I met with the social worker who'd been trying to help my folks take care of what had to be done after a death. She was appalled at the state of their memory. But she also said, "They are so sweet with each other. I hope when my husband and I are their age, we're like Jack and Ruthie."

When I helped my folks make important year-end financial decisions by phone, the woman who assisted us was especially kind and helpful. We told her how much we appreciated her and she responded, "You are the nicest people I've talked with all day!" My parents believe in treating others as they'd like to be treated.

When I visit, I sleep on the couch between their bedrooms. One night I watched them go back and forth between their bedrooms multiple times because they couldn't remember if they'd kissed each other good night. So sweet!

SAC-CORNEMUSE (SAILING WITH THE SCOTS GUARDS—A TRUE STORY)

Robbie Byrne

"Come on," shouted Lt. Cosgrove, the officer in charge of our sailing party, "Let's paint this town as red as their wine." So we did.

Myself, my Sac-Cornemuse (German for bagpipes) and ten members of the yacht, Contessa 3, had berthed an hour earlier in Cherbourg, France, and decided to try out the small wine bars around town. The captain of the Contessa, our company Sergeant-Major, decided to stay on board. The tide was in and he wanted to make the boat completely safe – safe enough to protect his hidden stock of Highland Whisky.

The trip had been organised as part of an Outward-Bound course for trainee soldiers of the Scots Guards. It was my first and, hopefully last trip aboard a sailing vessel. Irish landlubber I am – sailor I am not. I get seasick watching my bath fill up, and on this trip, I spent more time with my head overboard than enjoying the exhilarating roll of the boat.

After many hours of wine tasting (that was our excuse), someone in their wisdom shouted for the "piper" to pipe everyone back to the boat, which happened to be about two miles from the wine bar. Our party held each other up as they staggered and sang through the narrow streets (don't know who was holding me up – maybe the bagpipes). I started to play (it was 3 a.m.) when bedroom lights burst out of swinging shutters and French insults were thrown down at us like red-hot spears.

I kept on playing. Everyone else kept on staggering. Then a few words in pidgin English rose above the skirl of the pipes. "Why don't you lot go back to Scotland, haggis-bashers!" I wondered if he knew what a haggis was. "And take that wailing Octopus with you!"

As we approached the bottom of one narrow street – and I was running out of tunes to play – there stood a long line of dark shadows.

Shadows with arms and legs. The Gendarme. At least ten of them (well, it seemed like ten after all the wine we'd consumed).

More policemen stormed out of their vans dressed in riot gear: long sticks in one hand and revolvers in the other. I kept on playing. I thought, well, if I stop playing they might shoot me.

Visions of severed diplomatic relations (maybe severed limbs) and English Ambassadors being asked to vacate their embassies flashed through my mind, especially when someone behind me shouted: "We beat you at Waterloo, and that was …hic… before we even had a drink."

Quickly, I took a right turn and gave a rendition of "Scotland the Brave" just for good measure, as if to say "Party-poopers, we're not coming back to your country," and headed towards the docks and safety. We approached the jetty; everyone took the stone steps leading down to the berth, but in my drunken stupor I had forgotten that what comes in usually goes out, like for example, the tide. And over I went – bagpipes and all.

The sound of my bagpipes - like that of a thousand squealing cats in competition with an equal number of Banshees - filled the cool, summer French night air as I fell twenty feet or more, down onto the wooden pontoon beside the jetty that wasn't there anymore.

The gendarmes were laughing all the way back to their vans. I can't remember much about the fall, except a floating sensation and then a heavy thud, and then a voice saying: "What's wrong with using the steps like everyone else, you tosser."

I unwrapped the bagpipes from around my neck; the blow-stick was still in my mouth; the sheepskin bag gave a last, dying squeal, then I hobbled my way back to the Contessa.

The following night we set sail for Cowes (just off southern England. We stayed on board all day and kept a low profile). The night sea was covered with a thick mist. Everyone had a pulsating headache and I had a throbbing ankle. We took it in turns to navigate and work the tiller. When my turn arrived, the crew was sound asleep in their cosy bunks. A herring gull flew out of the mist and came within two feet of me, took one gawking look and then soared away into the nothingness. I was sure it had winked at me. The silence and creepy mist made me imagine all sorts of weird things. I glanced at the compass – I was supposed to keep my eye on it at all times, but that seagull kept diving over my head, and I couldn't concentrate – it must have been a French gull out for revenge.

I was so busy fighting off the bird to notice the massive black shape emerge out of the mist – until it was too late. The white cliffs of the "Needles" suddenly appeared. I was wrong – it was an English Seagull.

I started to panic. For God's sakes, I'm only a piper. What do I know about navigating a boat! The captain appeared from below deck – whisky bottle dangling out of his coat pocket. His mouth dropped open when he spotted the massive cliffs, grabbed the tiller, and steered like crazy to get us back on course. Vast black shapes like the stooping shoulders of giants loomed over us; foam hit the rocks below the cliffs and swept back over the edge of the boat. I hung onto the main mast until we were safely back on course.

Later that morning I piped the Contessa 3 into Cowes Harbour. Tourists (I hoped there weren't any French among them) and dock-workers peered and stared at us. Some of them even cheered.

Lt. Cosgrove ordered the crew to stand to attention on deck. He shouted above the skirl of the pipes: "Stand up proud, lads. You're Scots Guards. And, this time, piper – use the f…….. steps."

FICTION

Andrew

Gay Chambers

Only a blur of movement caught her eye as people scurried about. The rhythmic thump of the huge people-lift echoed through the massive room. It sounded like a heartbeat, steady and strong.

Throughout the day, she felt herself sync up with the machine as it rotated its clamshell pods in the immense steel structure. She watched people step off and rush away to places unknown. Some exited the lift with a bewildered look, seeking familiar faces. Scanning the crowd, they would break into a smile and wave as a friend swooped in with a hug.

It's been years since the war, but they still want to live down here. What I wouldn't give for a soft warm breeze.

The petite doctor scanned the area again. *Why did they place the clinic here of all places? It's out in the open with nothing to denote boundaries, nor are there any privacy walls. Just rows of beds and exam tables lined up like graves, half of them full already*. Finding the cleanest part of her sleeve, she wiped sweat off her brow. *Too much noise and too many people. It's hard to concentrate.*

She took a moment to check out the queue as they lined up against the grimy, yellow-tiled wall. Some leaning, some sitting, but most stood, shoulders slumped in hopelessness with misery lining their faces.

Feeling a presence, she looked down. Standing before her was a blonde-headed boy maybe 10 or 11 years old, holding a battered paper bag.

"Please, ma'am can you help him?"

I know he's considered non-essential, but I just can't send him away. His eyes pleaded with her.

Grabbing her clipboard, she asked, "What's your name?"

"Andrew, ma'am."

"Well Andrew, I don't know if I can help until I see him."

"Yes ma'am, please, he's all I got."

The thump of the machine dwindled into the background as he opened the bag and gently lifted out a small, filthy rag. The doctor flinched, thinking of all the nasty bugs clinging to it. She shuddered then opened the rag with trepidation. There lay a squirrel with his eyes closed, his chest rising with each breath. It didn't take long to see the problem. A terrible gash had opened one of his tiny legs from the hip to the knee.

"He needs stitches. Will he bite if I touch him?"

"Don't know. He hasn't bit anyone yet, but he's messed up right now."

"I'll give him something so he won't feel the stitching, but you'll need to hold him."

Andrew gently laid his finger on the little squirrel's chest. With the other hand, he stroked the tiny head.

"Go ahead, ma'am he knows I'm here."

She took the syringe and pushed the needle into the muscle. The little squirrel shifted but didn't open his eyes. The doctor touched his chest and could feel a fast strong heartbeat.

"Andrew," how did this happen?"

"We was playing over by that big old dead tree, you know the one by the side of the…"

"Doctor, Doctor over here," an attendant called out.

She looked up, "I'm in the middle of something. Go ahead and start, I'll be there in a minute."

"But Doctor…"

"I said just a minute." Turning back to Andrew, "We need to be quick about this. I don't know if he'll feel it or not. So hold on tight."

She threaded the needle and pulled the muscle together. The squirrel didn't move. *Good.* She quickly stitched it up then moved to the skin.

"Doctor, please," called the attendant. She didn't even look up, just kept stitching. When she was done, she wiped her brow again. *It's too hot in here.* She glanced up but nothing was out of the ordinary.

Covered in black bar-like cages, the lights barely radiated enough to reduce the shadows in the far corners. The vaulted ceiling, embedded with dirt-encrusted glass, rose high above, but only a small fraction of daylight showed through. *Sure would help if they'd clean them occasionally.*

She looked again at the stitches. "I don't know if he'll be able to use his leg, but that's the best I can do," she replied.

"Thank you Doctor. At least he has a chance."

Wrapping his leg, she said, "I'll give him some antibiotics to keep it from getting infected but you must keep him clean. Here wrap him in this cloth. When he wakes up use this syringe and feed him some milk every two hours."

A low rumble rippled beneath their feet. Fear spread across Andrew's face. The sudden blare of alarms blasting out of old metal discs near the ceiling made him jump. It had been years since they had emitted such a terrible sound. The ground rolled again. Tiles on the wall shattered and showered shards down on the people. The horrendous grinding screech of metal on metal clashed with the alarms as the huge people lift groaned to a halt.

All eyes turned to look upon their lifeline to the surface. Suspended, motionless, and eight feet off the ground, the clamshell gate was only halfway opened.

The sudden stop had thrown the passengers off their feet. Quickly the men crawled to peer over the ledge. One of them began to gesture. The women, holding their crying children, shook their heads.

I don't think they like his idea.

With shock, the doctor watched as the men, two at a time, moved closer to the lip and slipped over the edge. They dangled for a second, then dropped.

Standing up, they coaxed the women to lower their children. The mothers gently kissed their foreheads, laid down, held the children under their arms, and let go.

However, others in a closed pod weren't so lucky to escape. The screams were faint next to clangor of the alarm, and fists pounding on the metal walls sounded like dull thuds.

Realization struck those waiting for loved ones to descend. They weren't getting off. Like a wave, they rushed, pushed and shoved each other out of their way trying to reach the base of the lift.

I wish they'd shut off that alarm. Looking down, she saw Andrew was mesmerized with the scene on the lift.

"Andrew, quick take these," she shouted.

He turned to look up at her when he heard his name. "What happened?"

"I don't know, but I feel something bad is coming." The doctor held out some bandages for him.

"You need to get out of here. Go to the kitchen; there's a stairwell that heads to the surface."

Andrew stood looking around in fear and unbelief. Another ripple rolled under them nearly toppling the two over.

"Andrew, move it."

He grabbed the bandages and stuffed them into the paper bag. Gently lifting his squirrel now wrapped in a clean cloth, he took off slipping in and out of the scurrying group of people.

The doctor watched as the slim figure scurried around the corner into the hall that led to the kitchen.

I wonder if I'll ever see Andrew again.

GRIEVING ANGEL

Janet Skibinski

The overcast sky filled with rolling dirty grey clouds promised rain later in the day. A chill circled the neighborhood. The green pop-up shelter covered the two dozen tan, metal folding chairs that sat on an all-weather carpet. A microphone and stand, a bucket of fresh dirt, and a basket filled with yellow roses were at the front of the chairs.

The grieving angel mounted on an infant's grave watched as mourners entered Saint Malachi's Church. The bell rang a lonely bong. The sounds of *Amazing Grace* could be heard drifting through the doors when they opened.

The stone angel thought how lucky the human was to be at eternal peace. *Another soul is entering the Lord's home. Praise be to God Almighty!* She could only stay posed prone over the innocent babe's resting place for all time.

The angel appeared to smile as the hymns were heard softly through the cracks in the church's walls. Peace, peace forever. *God rest the eternal soul.*

Two men in black suits came out of Saint Malachi's and prepared to roll the simple wood coffin to the adjoining grave yard. Father O'Malley sprinkled holy water on the last bed the deceased would occupy as altar boys waved containers of smoking incense around it. Six nuns dressed all in black from their calf-length dresses to their stockings and lace-up shoes surrounded the coffin, acting as pall bearers.

Father O'Malley, Mrs. Margaret Montgomery, three women who favored Mrs. Montgomery in looks, their husbands, and an old gentleman using a cane were next in the procession. The rest of the mourners exited the church. Some parishioners stopped to express their concern for the family now that Sister Rose was gone. Others questioned if there would be a reception after the burial.

"How did she die?" a parishioner asked.

"Someone told me she starved herself to death."

"That girl was always doing for others, never thinking of herself. We've lost a saint today."

When all were seated, Father O'Malley began. "Mrs. Montgomery, Bridget, Maura, Priscilla and husbands, Mr. Montgomery, and family and friends of Sister Rose Montgomery, welcome to a celebration of life! Halleluiah, Sister Rose is home with Our Precious Lord! Halleluiah!" An echo of halleluiahs could be heard across the cemetery.

Grieving Angel listened to all the lovely words the priest spoke. He told how he and Sister Rose had grown up together, were best friends, and even thought they would marry one day. But God had other plans for them. Both were called to serve the Lord as priest and nun. After several more sentimental statements, someone cleared their throat.

"Father, I want to say something!" Mrs. Montgomery stood up and started for the microphone.

"Of course, Maggie."

"Rose was my special child. I love all me girls, but Rose…she almost wasn't born. I have held my shame inside for far too many years. Now that my Rose is with the Lord, the truth can be told." Tears formed in Maggie's eyes. Her face turned a faint red. She cleared her throat once again. "I came to this country seeking something better than I had in me own beloved country, Ireland. 'T was one of the most difficult decisions I made. I never saw me mam or da again." Pausing to wipe her eyes and nose, she continued. "I had no skills, but Paddy O'Shea gave me a job in his pub pullin' beer and waitin' tables. That's where I met Michael, the best man God ever put on this earth. There was only one problem. Michael's parents didn't like me. I was a dirty Irish spud digger."

At this the old man with the cane stood. He turned to leave. The mourners looked at him in disbelief and the buzz of their gossiping filled the silence.

"Oh, no, you don't, Mr. Montgomery. You aren't getting' out of it this time!" Maggie's green eyes blazed with all the hurt she held inside for years. "I'm not meaning to air no dirty laundry, but this needs to be said.

After Michael and I were wed, there came a knock on me door one day. There stood Mr. Malcolm Montgomery. I asked what he wanted. He asked how much money would I take to divorce his son. I tried to shut the door in his face, but he shoved in, grabbed me arm and dragged me into the bedroom. I will leave the rest up to you to surmise. Shortly after, signs showed that I was with child. I didn't know what to do. I wanted a baby so badly, but not one that was a bastard!" Maggie shook reliving the pain. "I went to see Monsignor Riley and confessed it all. He assured me the baby was a blessing, a gift from God, it was meant to be. Seven months later, me sweet, precious, special Rose was born."

Malcolm Montgomery looked around. "You don't believe this ignorant woman, do you? You know how the Irish lie. How they cheat. How they can't stay sober long enough to do a decent day's work!" He turned and leaving the graveside pounded his cane on the ground with each step he took. All eyes were on his back until Maggie began again.

"I told you all this story because I want you to know that when things look their darkest 'tis when God is putting His plan together to save you. Rose was not wanted, but, oh my, what a special joy she was! I love all me girls and each has given me more pleasure than I ever imagined possible. But Rose…Rose was never meant to be, so she has returned home to her true Father and Maker. God, bless and keep her in Your arms for eternity."

Maggie went to the coffin, placed a last kiss on it, picked up a handful of dirt and threw it into the empty pit, then gently tossed in

Rose's favorite flower—a yellow rose. One by one, the others followed. Father O'Malley was the last to leave. He, too, kissed the coffin. As he turned to leave, Grieving Angel saw the mist forming in his eyes. She watched as he walked slowly towards the priest's home. Tears appeared to flow from her eyes and rain continued throughout the day.

DORIS

Lois Henry

Doris came churning around the corner, hips so wide they seemed to turn on separate axles, and smiled broadly at me.

The other waitress had called in sick so Doris would fill in until Gino showed up to help me with the dinner rush.

I'd never worked with Doris before. She was usually leaving as I was coming on.

Sometimes, she would have a drink at the counter with Tito, the owner, their white bouffant hairdos competing for air space.

After a while, Tito would wave his hand, gold bracelet flashing. "Dorees! Time to go home!"

She'd slug down the rest of her drink, smudging her fire-engine-red lipstick, and toddle off.

Rude, I thought.

Gino, the smug, lanky night waiter with his "Italian stallion" necklace, was worse, calling Doris "that old cow" loud enough for her to hear.

I felt sorry for her.

She could be someone's grandma. OK, a grandma with a distracting amount of cleavage and badly glued false eyelashes.

Still, she was an elder. Show some respect.

It was a Thursday, and we caught a good crowd early.

We were nowhere in the weeds — at least I wasn't.

But Doris was sweating. The big red smile gone. Pretty soon she was swearing and using those hips like a snowplow if I got between her and the bread drawer.

She seemed confused, exchanging soups for salads so often we were short on bowls.

I started running bread and waters to her tables.

Then more — fresh coffees; extra parm; where's the salt? No one ever brought my cheese bread; Miss, I ordered milk with my dinner (Seriously? You're like 50!)

Now, I was starting to swear, especially when I saw her scooping up my tips.

"Uh, Doris, that was my table," I said.

"I brought the wine," she growled.

"Only because I was busy with your tables in the back!"

"Hey! What goin' on?! Customer can hear!" Tito's shiny pink shirt strained over his second-trimester belly as he scowled at us.

"Little Miss thinks I shouldn't get a cut of her tips for helping her customers," Doris said.

"Doris help you?" Tito demanded.

"Yeah, but I've…"

"I don' wanna hear," he said. "Doris help you, you give her some tip. I don' wanna hear no more!"

I glared at Doris, who smirked. Smirked? Grandmas don't smirk!

More Thursday diners were streaming in when Gino, thank God for that arrogant goomba with his too-tight pants, finally showed up.

I filled Gino in as Doris clocked out. I seethed while she sat next to Tito, counting her tips – my tips.

"Ha! Ha! I thought you loved that old Doris. That old mucca," Gino teased. "Now you know."

I brought Tito another drink and Doris leaned her boob prow toward me.

"Pretty good night, eh, hon?"

I stared daggers. Tito shook his head at me and waved his hand in Doris's direction.

"Dorees! Time to go home!"

She gave me a smudgy, red-lipped smirk and toddled off.

DON'T NAME HIM CAMILLE

Richard Meeks

Jeanette Gagne stood at the kitchen counter shaking the coloring packet into the brick of Nucoa margarine she'd dumped in the mixing bowl. As she stirred the contents into a pale-yellow spread, she winked at her mother. "It may resemble butter when I finish, but it sure won't taste like it."

Sitting on the couch reading to her grandson, Helen nodded in assent. Gray-haired and reed thin, She had moved in to mind the baby during the day while her daughter was in the city working for Minneapolis Honeywell. Hard as it was to keep up because of her arthritis, it was worth it when Robert called her 'Gramma.'

Jeanette continued mixing, pushing her auburn hair back with her forearm. She put a tablespoon of the margarine into a paper cup, crushed in a Ritz cracker, and handed the snack and a plastic spoon to her son. "Careful now, Little Bob," she cautioned, "try not to spill any on the carpet."

She felt an inner glow watching the two-year-old gobble the treat. "He looks so much like his papa, with his brown eyes and that mop of hair. I see Camille whenever I look at him. It's what gets me through the week downtown." Her face clouded. "I'd give anything to know where Cam is and what he's doing. It's been ages since I got a letter from him."

"And Little Bob has never seen him," Helen added, shaking her head.

Jeanette thought for a moment. "Just before Cam left for overseas, he called me from Fort Benning. I was home from the hospital with Robert for a few days. They'd promised him a furlough after finishing training, but he told me the army was shipping out his unit immediately. I blubbered over the phone and said, 'Guess you won't be able to see our boy.' I was wearing the necklace he had given me when we were dating, and the baby caught his finger in the clasp and bawled. So I was glad Camille could leave knowing at least he'd heard his son cry."

Her mother laid the picture book, *Make Way for Ducklings,* on the coffee table, and asked, "Was he disappointed you didn't name the baby after him?"

Jeanette's face lit up. "It may be okay for French-Canadian boys, but my husband's last words were, 'Whatever you do, don't name him Camille.'"

Helen rose from the couch and switched on the ceiling fan. "It's too hot inside. Let's go sit on the porch. I'd make us some sweet tea, but we've used up our ration for the month. When the Good Humor man comes by, we'll get ice cream."

When he heard the magic words, Robert sprang up and performed a Lilliputian dance of joy.

Helen watched him waddle outside to wait for the white truck, then gave her daughter a questioning look. "When is a door not a door?"

"When it's ajar," Jeanette responded, sighing. "That thing hasn't shut right since Cam left. He would have fixed it when he got leave. At least it keeps Little Bob busy swatting at flies that get in."

They followed the baby out to the shaded air on the porch. Helen winced as she tried to get comfortable in her wicker rocking chair. Jeanette saw her struggle and said, "You need a cushion, Mom. Keep an eye on the boy, and I'll fix you right up."

Her mother pressed a finger to her smiling lips and asked, "Honey, while you're inside, would you turn on the radio so we can listen to the news?" As Helen watched Robert scoot around on his hands and knees, her eyes moved to the two framed pictures in the window. The first was a color photograph of Camille in his 82nd Airborne jumpsuit standing by a C-47 plane. Beside it, a certificate with a blue star on a red-and-white border proved to the world that this family had someone in The Service.

In the house, Jeanette picked up her favorite pillow and carried it over to where, anchored in the parlor like the Rock of Gibraltar, sat the big Philco console radio. She twisted the knob, adjusted the volume, and returned to the porch.

"Put this behind you, Mom," she said, handing Helen the pillow. "It's given me a lot of comfort."

Covered in a GI military red with gold fringe, the pillow's case read: US ARMY. Beneath that:

For My Wife

Love unending warm and true

Sweetheart mine this brings to you

Love that hopes that Happiness

All your days may cheer and bless

"I recall when you got this," Helen said, admiring the inscription.

"It's one of my favorite things," Jeanette professed, her eyes misting. "Cam sent it last year from Georgia. This pillow, my necklace, his letters—and most of all, Robert—are all I have to remember him by. Now he's jumping from airplanes into who knows what."

Helen looked again at Cam's photo. "Well, we know he survived D-Day. That was in June, and… Oh! Gabriel Heatter's coming on. Let's listen."

Mother and Daughter settled into their chairs as the veteran newsman's calm voice wafted through the screen door.

Ah, there's good news tonight. The latest dispatches from the BBC show that the French invasion continues to be a success. Allied paratroopers have been landing near the Rhine River since Tuesday morning, and General Eisenhower says…

They listened as they waited for the ice cream wagon to make its daily rounds. Gramma was the first to spot the truck raising dust a block away. She stood, squinting at the approaching vehicle. "Why doesn't he ring his bell? Can't be the mailman. There's no delivery on Sundays."

The truck stopped in front of their house. A uniformed Western Union employee slid out and approached the porch.

The stocky, balding man removed his gray cap, looked at both women, and then spoke to Jeanette. "Are you Mrs. Gagne? I have this telegram for you… Are you going to be all right?"

Married at seventeen, the young mother stood up, an apple-sized lump forming in her throat, and mumbled, "Oh, sure, I'm okay."

Helen hurried over and asked, "What does it say, Honey?"

"It's, it's… from the War Department—maybe Cam's wounded." Jeanette's hands shook as she tore open the yellow envelope. It began: *THE SECRETARY OF WAR DESIRES ME TO EXPRESS HIS DEEP REGRET…*

That's as far as she read. Tears blinded her vision as Helen wrapped her in a sobbing embrace. The Western Union man took a step forward. "Ma'am, if uh, there's anything I can do…?"

The older woman shook her head and led her daughter and grandson back into the house.

The messenger remained on the porch for a time, feeling helpless. Turning to leave, he spotted the picture frames in the front window, and came over to examine Cam's photo and the blue star certificate. On impulse, he snapped to attention and held a long salute. Then he replaced his hat, returned to his truck and drove away.

The telegram lay crumpled beside the screen door, which swayed back and forth in the muggy air.

GRAND OLE' FISH AND CHIPS

Robbie Byrne

I know what we can do," says Sam as we walk through the town center on a cool summer's night.

"Find something to eat," I say.

"Well, yes, but there's no way I'm paying for it."

"You're gonna steal?"

"Listen, a mate of my brother works in the bakery and he says they load up and store their cakes in vans overnight and deliver them to the shops the next day."

"My dad says stealing is for losers."

"Come on, Josh," says Sam mischievously. "No one will find out. All we have to do is crawl under the back fence and nip into the vans and hey, cakes galore."

"I don't know," I say, nervously, "those cakes belong to someone."

"Their insurance will cover it. Ah, come on, Josh. It'll be a piece of cake."

And that's Sam. Always wanting a slice of something without earning it—like working a paper or milk round like the rest of us. I've known Sam for a few months now and he knows he isn't allowed anywhere near my father's doorstep until he stops his thievery.

We head for the bakery on the other side of town. Near the bottom of a narrow lane is a wire fence and beyond that are at least ten bakery vans.

"You first," I say to Sam. He crawls beneath the fence and I follow.

We creep like raiding commandos towards the first van, stand up and open the door. "Enough cakes here to feed the town. We can sell them cheap and make ourselves some cash, Josh, me boy."

We grab about ten boxes each and run down to the fence, crawl back under it dragging the boxes with us, stand up and come face to face with a policeman.

"Doing a bit of exercise are we, lads," says the tall, broad-shouldered copper.

"Yes, erm, no," says Sam, "We found these boxes lying around and thought we'd take them down to the cop-shop."

"You mean the police station, lad?"

"I think it's terrible the way folks just throw their trash all over the place, so we thought we could clean the place up a bit, yer know, do our bit for the community."

"I see," says the copper, and frowns at us with thick long eyebrows. He looks like a bald eagle. He's also cock-eyed and I'm not too sure if he's looking at me or Sam.

"Well, why don't we take a visit to the 'cop-shop.' We can help the community even more by keeping you young buggers off the streets."

With that we are frog-marched (what does that mean?) back through the center of town and into the cop-shop, taken to a windowless room and told to sit at a desk. There is a telephone on the desk. We wait and wait.

"I wish I had a cake to eat," says Sam.

"Shut up," I say, "you've got us in enough trouble as it is."

"My da's gonna kill me," says Sam. "My mother will suffocate me. And my brother will practice his kick-boxing on me. And my sister …"

"You think you've got it bad," I say. "My da will not only murder me he'll wallop me with his leather belt and that's worse than death."

"But you've got the Bible, remember," says Sam, "keeps your ass safe."

"I did have the Bible 'till me da figured out why he was whipping me and there wasn't a genuine tear in sight. He threw the Bible away."

"Wow, you're dead," says Sam.

The cock-eyed, eagle-browed copper enters the room, sits down in front of us and takes out a pen from his inside pocket. He glares at Sam and stares at me, or it could be the other way around, I'm not sure.

"Now. You," he says, as he writes something in his notebook.

"Me?" I say.

"No. Him," says the copper.

"Me?" says Sam.

"Am I looking at you?"

"I'm not sure," says Sam.

"Don't be impertinent. Now. What's your name?

"Who me?" I say.

"No. Father frigging Christmas. Who do you think?"

"But you're looking at him," I say.

"Looking at whom?" says the copper.

"Sam," says I.

"So, your first name is Sam. What's your last name?"

"My name is Joshua," I say.

"But you just said your name is Sam.

"No. He's Sam, I'm Joshua."

"Okay. Let's keep this simple. Let's start again."

"What's your first and last name?"

"Who? Me or Joshua?

"What's your problem, lad?" says the copper.

"Which one of us are you frigging looking at?

"Don't you dare use such language in this station, young man," says the cock-eyed, eagle-looking eyebrow.

"You, boy, go stand over there out of the way."

Sam stands, scrapes his chair on the stone-tiled floor and walks over to the corner of the room.

"Face the corner."

Sam turns and faces the corner like a naughty schoolboy.

"Now," says eagle face. "What is your first and last name?"

"Joshua Hanley," I say calmly.

"Good. And your middle name?"

"My mother calls me, Sarcastic."

"Listen, boy. You may think this is all a laugh, a game, but believe me, laddie, when I get through writing this report you two will definitely get a year's holiday in a nice little paradise called Juvenile Hall, otherwise known as hell on earth."

"Hey. You," says the copper.

Me?" says Sam, still facing the corner.

"Yes, you. Sit down."

Sam plonks himself down on the hard, wooden chair.

"Now. What's your first name?"

"Sam."

"Last name?"

"O'Neil."

"Middle name?"

Sam is silent for a few moments.

"Middle name?"

"It's the same as that Irish show presenter on the Late Late show," says Sam, "have you heard of him?"

"Irish show … what are you talking about. All I'm asking for is your middle name."

"He's famous in Ireland," says Sam. "You must have heard of him, surely, his last name is Byrne."

"WHAT'S YOUR MIDDLE NAME?" I hear footsteps in the hallway, maybe someone thinks we're being murdered in here.

"Josh. Promise me you won't laugh."

"I won't laugh," I say.

"My middle name is Gay," he says.

I don't laugh.

The phone rings.

"Hello," says the policeman. "Yes. I see. Okay. I'll send him out. Hey. You."

"Me?" says Sam.

"Your father's outside waiting for you. Good luck."

Sam gives me a terrifying glance as he slides out the door. I kinda half-smile back at him.

I sit in silence as the cock-eyed copper writes something in his notepad. Every time I open my mouth to utter something he raises his hand; I clam up.

"Right. You were about to say?"

"I don't think Sam will steal again."

"Learnt his lesson, eh. Hope so."

He stands, glances at his notepad.

"Dad?"

"Yes, son?"

"Why are you so smart?"

"Guess it's part of being Irish. What's for dinner?"

"Irish stew."

"I hate Irish stew. Here, let's surprise your mother and grab some fish and chips on the way home, eh. How's that sound?"

"That sounds grand," I say, "Just grand."

No More Riddles

Rose Wilstead

Mom shuffled around in my room while I pretended to sleep. It was better this way. I couldn't do it again. Being the dumbest kid in school was hard enough but, in the county, no—I couldn't do it. Not today.

"Your friends are waiting." Mom knew I wasn't sleeping.

"For what?" I kept my eyes closed.

"The game. They're waiting outside for *the* game." Mom tugged my blankets off the bed. She rolled her eyes, irritated that I was giving up.

"What game?" I asked, miffed with both my mom and the world.

"You know which game." The annual fair hosted a riddles obstacle course, more riddles and less obstacles. They allowed two "lucky" competitors to play. Most of my friends, and those who weren't, wanted to be a competitor but every year, no matter how hard I tried to *not* play, I was always picked.

Mom thought solving riddles would help my brain develop. She was wrong, they made my brain twist in pain, dying a slow, agonizing death.

I walked out of my now gloomy room and saw three of my friends in the living room. Mom was way ahead of me. She'd played her hand well. Winning the games, would ease your life as well.

"Back, again," Seth said, although it sounded like a question.

"Yeah, I guess so." I shot Mom a look but she suddenly started cleaning the kitchen.

"Your mother said you wanted to come with us." Kawe threw an arm around my neck.

Seth gave Kawe a high five, then turned his tiny hands toward me. It looked like a giant trying to thumb wrestle with a ladybug. I was by far the largest, always.

It felt like hours until we finally made it to the fair's parking lot. A black, dreary trailer stood in the middle with a sign that read, *The Trailer of Riddles.*

I stood by the car, petrified. Kawe dragged me across the fair and soon, we came to the edge of the stage. Asmiza with her long dark hair, jumped up and down with excitement.

She was pretty. I was dumb. That's why she used to be my crush.

I'd outgrown her, I told myself. I told myself this a lot lately.

A woman stood in the center of the stage and listed the rules but I didn't listen. It didn't matter.

"Now who would like to challenge the Trailer of Riddles?" The woman asked, the growing crowd raised their hands—everyone but me. She frowned and pointed directly at me. "You."

Asmiza gave me a sympathetic look and stepped in front of me. "I'll take his place."

The woman on stage shook her head and taunted, "Don't be a chicken, boy."

Hands from the crowd pushed me forward. I would show the world my failings. Again.

"Her too!" the woman shouted, now pointing at Asmiza.

My old crush mouthed *sorry* before walking on stage next to me. Men in black suits lined the edge of the stage, cutting off the crowd from entering onto the stage—or keeping us on, I hadn't decided which.

"To win, one contestant must solve all the riddles *and* escape before the timer runs out." The woman paused, pushing down the button of the glass timer. Walls slammed down around us, cutting the stage down to a tiny, dark room. On the other side of the wall, she yelled to the crowd, "The game starts now!"

Lights flickered on. Asmiza and I were nearly touching in an enclosed room, barely big enough for our teenaged bodies.

A note pinned to the wall in front of us, read *The more you take, the more I leave behind. What am I?*

The intercom speaker above us crackled to life. "Players, thirty seconds."

"This one's easy. Footsteps," Asmiza answered.

The door unlocked, swinging open.

"Correct!" the intercom answered.

It was too easy. I stared at her back until I realized she'd gone through three more doors. I caught up with her just as she read the next riddle, "Every day people from all over the world come and visit me but not for long. I am considered by many to be very dirty yet few people want to live without me. Whenever people come see me, they reveal a part of themselves they rarely show others. What or who am I?"

I stumbled into the room, not ready to humiliate myself again. Every year, the same outcome. My heart raced. For months, the local news replayed last year's losing question.

"Look," Asmiza elbowed me and gestured to the replica bathroom in front of us. "They reveal a part of themselves they rarely show others. Get it?"

"A hotel?" It was happening again. My head turned to mush. Thoughts swam in circles. Last year, all I had to say was my name and I couldn't do it. My hands were sweaty. These games, they did nothing but make me look stupid.

"We can live without hotels, but we can't live without what?" She waited, her big blue eyes sparkled. She nodded her head in the direction of the toilet.

"Toilet?"

"Correct," the overcome bellowed. "Find the clue."

Correct. I was—or rather Asmiza was—correct.

"Where do you think they put the clue?" Asmiza smiled wide, she probably already knew the answer.

I ran my fingers along the lip of the toilet bowl. An object fell into my hand and I held it up for Asmiza.

"It's a key!" She clapped her hands together but didn't take the key. She motioned toward the thin door behind the toilet—meant for much smaller teenagers than me. "Go, go!"

"But you—"

"*Go!*"

I shoved the key into the lock and hurried through, covering my eyes from the bright overhead lights.

"Last test," the speaker boomed. "Look for the exit. It starts with *t*, is filled with *t* and ends with *t.*"

My eyes adjusted to the room, revealing a kitchenette. I looked back at the skinny door and wished that Asmiza had snuck through.

"Make some tea!" Her muffled voice came through the wall.

"Make some tea," I repeated. With shaky hands, I walked to the teapot and boiled the water.

"Eight minutes left," the speaker warned.

Pouring the water into the teacup, I noticed words at the bottom, "I can see you but you can't see me."

"Louder," Asmiza ordered.

I turned but before obeying, I saw the floor-length mirror. The same mirrors on my mom's crime shows. Rushing toward the wall, I pushed against the mirror and heard a click. The mirror swung back and I stumbled out.

"Congratulations!" the woman exclaimed.

A second later, Asmiza ran toward me and hugged me—as a former crush.

"Why did you help me?" I asked her; she could have won. And won easily.

She blushed and grabbed my hand. "You didn't need me when it really counted."

She wasn't my former crush. And I wasn't the dumbest kid in town.

POETRY

ANKE HODENPIJL

Being Boreal

A silvered crescent moon smiles
on a glittering glacial meadow below.
Silent wolves gaze at the arctic hinterland
head erect, ears pulled forward
convinced of their divinity
cocksure of nightfall's oracle.

In the distance,
past the haze of shadows,
a blue-black horizon blushes with a frosty glow,
bearing witness to the swelling overstep of prospectors
where worth is measured in gold, oil and ownership,
indifferent to First Nation Wisdom.

A quiver of nocturnal green
fondles the infinite stillness
then evaporates like a melting mirage
foreshadowing a greater apparition.
My desire broods like that of a young, inexperienced lover.
Will this be the night?
Will I be with her?
Will I be satisfied?

Suddenly,
she explodes across the night sky
dancing with a kaleidoscopic hocus-pocus
of emerald, rose, blond and lilac.
I listen to the silence,
I hear the ancient Grandmothers
inspiring her antics
as she smears the heavens with her joy.
Her name is Aurora
Her song is her own
Her light is within
Now within me,
I am.

Annis Cassells

Resilience

I.

The crush comes swiftly
suffocating,
devastating.
In that moment
of fragility,
of vulnerability,
frenzied heart thumps,
pumping blood
to your uncomprehending brain.
The crush lifts slowly.
It just takes time.
Watch for the return of life,
not as you once knew it
but new
and good.

II.

You begin to rise.
And if you can't
yet stand tall
step forward
or feint sideways,
dig into the earth
with one elbow

then the other.
Drag yourself an inch or two ahead
like the downed soldier you are.
Whatever it takes
know you are enough.
Watch for the return of life,
not as you once knew it
but new and good
and worth the effort
Baby steps
or inch-by-inch
it's all forward.

III.

And in that moment
when passion returns,
overruns the heart's
hysteria,
overtakes
the clouded-over brain,
you see the light,
the path to acceptance
to peace
within yourself.
You know you are
enough
to overcome
whatever
comes.

The Practice

I grasp the purple yoga mat's edge
recognize the familiar texture
inhale its rubbery scent.
One practiced motion unfurls
my island of focus
of meditation
of peace.
On this lavender oasis,
sanctuary
for introspection
vessel of reverence,
while soul-to-sole
in sun salutations
I set my solitary
Intention.

BRENT GILL

The Auction

The auctioneer's song has a magical sound.
And drama comes if the buyers abound.
Bidding's not done as an obvious thing,
Disinterest to all. Let the auctioneer sing.
My son had raised his first 4-H steer.
This calf off our ranch was something to cheer.
Feeding and grooming, then brought him to sell.
For a 10-year-old boy, he'd done quite well.
Dad and I watched as he washed and curried,
His uniform on, it was then time to hurry.
The boy and his calf got into the line.
We leaned on a tree, and could see just fine.
The calf was fat and the boy filled with pride,
A thousand pound beef - a tenth that beside.
Grampa was there, this steer to buy.
A pox on anybody else who'd try.
"Less'n a half" Dad cautioned me
"But twenty'd be a good price to see.
I wanna buy it, but not for too high.
You watch for who's biddin', others may try."
The auctioneer knew who'd start the sale,
Gramps' hat gave a tip, his only hail.
The bidding was on and began at a buck.
This calf was his, with any luck.
But out of Dad's sight, my bid went wingin'.
"A nickel" said the auctioneer's singin'.

As soon as I bid, I looked, actin' bugged.
"Who bid", Gramps barked. "I dunno." I shrugged.
With an ever-so-subtle tip of his hat,
Dad silently said "Here, buddy, take that!"
The bid was raised to a dollar and a dime.
Then my thumb raised that bid one more time.
Gramps jumped nearly out of his skin.
He mumbled an oath, very unlike him.
I'd taken the bid to a buck fifteen,
The next bid is twenty. His price it'd seem.
A wave of his hand, he took it to twenty.
"No more now, that's a great plenty.
That's my grandson, can't they see?"
He just didn't know the bidder was me.

I let the auction go a little bit more.
But my final bid was a nickel more.
A big wave of Gramp's hand for all to see,
Nothing subtle, he yelled, "A Buck Thir-tee!"
The auctioneer sang "A dollar and thirty.
Thank ya there boys. That went really purty."
"Didja see who was biddin?" Dad asked of me.
"No, sir I didn't. I never could see!"

CARLA MARTIN,

Ode to My Music and Piano

I slip my fingers onto
the ivory and ebony keys.
They are cool and smooth
to the touch.
When pressed,
a sonorous sound
lifts into the sultry summer night
as fireflies flicker
under twilight trees

My eyes follow black patterns
dancing across the page.
My brain interprets
into lilting melodies
and strident chords.

Music!
Mysterious essence
that describes
the abandoned companion's pain
the conquering hero's joy
the new mother's love.
You waft into our ears
spiral up to our minds
pulling out memories
of Christmas Eves,
ocean waves,
and first kisses.
Under your sway
the lonely night
is filled,

the hardened heart
is softened,
wrong
is made right.
In your spell
the universe spins
and stars twinkle.
My feet press the pedals
that release vibrating strings.
Sound reverberates
through the dusk.
Fingers ache,
backbone strains,
yet my soul is soothed
after playing music
on my piano.

Ode to My Boots

I slip my feet into your
dove-like skins.
Soft suede
soothes my toes,
wraps my ankles
like a lover's hand
caressing a cheek.

When I step out
in these boots
I am coy
yet assured
brave
yet vulnerable.
Hard heels say
"Conqueror!"

Light gray leather says
"Lady!"

You fit me better
than the lousy loafers
worn in a pinched marriage.
My critical, miserly man
trampled my spirit.
It took all my strength
to limp away.

But beautiful boots
you have restored my confidence.
How exciting
to face the world
clad in your
impenetrable fortresses!
I can squash bugs
jump puddles
stride up to a new man
live with hope.

What was wounded
is now stronger than ever.
None can step on my toe
and bruise my soul.
I am invincible in you,
my boots.

Trees and Lovers

Trees send out roots
Roots sense where to find water
Where to avoid stones
Pierce the hard, unforgiving soil
Always searching
Deeply drinking nourishment

Providing stability
Enabling the tree to stand tall
You and I send out roots

We share our dreams
Our disappointments
Our joys
Piercing through the dark, turbulent tenor of our time
Always searching
Deeply drinking nourishment from each other's goodness
Providing stability
Holding hands
Joining bodies
Connecting souls
Growing branches of support
So we, too, can stand tall like trees
Reaching up to the heavens

Pebbles and Stones

Sometimes love is like pebbles in a stream
Jagged edges tumbling in the foaming water
Swirling and dancing in the turbulence
Born downstream in a whirlpool of desire
Pounded by the current
Barely coming up for air
Exploding into a thousand shards
Spinning towards the light

Sometimes love is like the tranquil stones
Sunk to the bottom of a lake
Once rough, now smooth
Released from the tumult of passion
Nestling quietly side by side
Gaining comfort in the stillness

Gazing at shafts of sunlight piercing the gloom
Remembering the whirlpool

Thankful to be resting
Listening to heartbeats
Becoming one with the deep

Judy Kukuruza

The Answer

To sleep deeply without fear—
In quiet, comfort, Peace—
To not feel rejection or pain,
But rather the comforting arms of Mother Ocean.

She does not judge, but welcomes.
There are no demands,
Only waves reaching out,
Pulling us back to her.

We will join her—
Let her depths swallow us
And our pain—and then,
We sleep in her bosom.

We sleep deeply without fear,
Without pain or heartache.
Our bleeding stops forever
And we are one with eternity.

Complement

The moon is filling,
Rounding himself with power and light.
Mother Ocean reaches up,
White caps and strong waves.

He throws his light everywhere;
She pulls it into her depths.
He laughs.
Her waves roil.

He lights her way
as her waters move to gently lap the sand;
His light spreading, reaching,
Her calming presence covering.

They are one.
The Universe smiles.

LaVerne Lovelady

The Poet Next Door

The jaundiced eye
 of the poet next door
sees jaded truth in
isolated circumstance.
She speaks of crass exclusion
 and being poor;
of the prejudiced high-brows
 of social segregation.
She speaks of out-door toilets
 and tin wash-tubs for bathing;
about absent, drunken fathers,
lost dreams, and mothers who
 slave in the well-heeled homes of others.
She speaks of judgment
 according to the tatters
 in a little girl's dress
 or by the holes
 in a pair of Sunday shoes.
She says "we people"
 couldn't possibly understand
      about such things as
           condemnation;
                about poverty
                     and shame.

I Am My Mother's Song

I Am My Mother's Song
My mother's song was born
the day my father left.
At first, it was a moaning
that rocked and groaned
before our council fire;
a quiet grieving,
birthing words
obscured within her soul;
shattered sound,
fractured words
I could not understand.
I muffled my ears
and stared into her eyes
until they smiled;
until the noxious noise
became a chant,
a muted melody,
a lullaby.
I am the moaning;
the groaning beside the fire.
I am the chant,
the melody,
the lullaby.
I am my mother's song!

MANDY WALLACE

Mario & Luigi

You're the 90s Luigi
To my Super Mario.
You and me, side by side.

Me: punching prize blocks for the level up.
Me: stealing Koopa shells to fly.
Me: stomping Goombas just to save us both.

And you: bouncin' along behind,
Doin' fuckin' nothin' to help.

Satisfied

I finish a poem and something
inside me that's always
gnawing gnawing gnawing gnawing
licks its lips and belches.

NELSON VARON

The Christmas Tree

Twinkling lights white red and green
Lit up the yearly Yuletide scene.
Douglas Firs of every size
Soon would brighten children's eyes.
One by one each tree was sold
Then carried off through the biting cold.
When all but one was sold that eve,
The owner was about to leave
When from the corner of his eye

He saw a homeless man nearby.
The owner asked, "Would you like this tree?"
"Not 'less you could give it to me."
"Well here then, Merry Christmas!" the owner said,
As he rushed to his warm home and bed.
The homeless man gazed at that tree.
On each branch he seemed to see
The ornaments, the bubble lights,
The tinsel, how he loved those nights
When as a boy so long ago
He'd wake up to that happy glow.
It mattered not the tree was bare
He saw such joyful memories there.
And now alone in the cold and dark,
His heart was warmed by the kind of spark
That lights the night when we believe
'T'is blessed to give and to receive.

PORTIA CHOI

Battleship Missouri

Lost in the bowel of a battleship
surrounded by steel walls and stairs,
I am alone,
breathing the musty air of past lives
cramped in a floating community:
offices with manual typewriters and file cabinets,
recreational room with wooden card tables and chairs,
kitchen with industrial-sized metal stove,
bedroom of metal bunks.

My footsteps echo the past:
    clicking of typewriter keys,
    shuffling of cards and laughter,
sizzling of bacon and clanking of spatulas,
creaking of bunkbeds and nasaled snoring.
My breath intermingles with memories of boys and men
sailing to fight for freedom
on the Pacific Ocean waves.

Cranes

Thousands of cranes flutter
from the ashes of war.
They ascend higher and
higher joined by more cranes,
flying upward over
a rainbow, finding peace.

SHELLEY EVANS

Expression of My Art

The sunset's unforgettable in my rear-view mirror
Tonight; the presence of God's spirit is here.
Inspirational beams of light illuminate the sky
With radiance. It almost makes me cry.

Instead, I sigh.

I sigh in awe of the ultimate painter, God,
Whose brushwork is so wondrous I applaud.
He colors the horizon in brilliant expression,
A kaleidoscopic palette full of passion.

It's smashin'!

This smashin' exhibit of the Creator's view
Of His world in every imaginable hue
Is enough to stimulate my poetic sentiment
Into a composition of words that represent

My intent.

My intent to create *a*rises from my heart
Which I implement to orchestrate my art
By rhyming adjectives, verbs, and nouns
Until they reproduce lyrical sounds.

Poetry abounds.

Poetry abounds in my expression of
How I feel, swaddled in God's love.
His love is absolute, exactly what I need
To be all He has made me, to succeed.

Indeed.

The Beach is My Heart's Home

Today we drove from Bakersfield
Headed for Pismo Beach.
I am ever thankful that
The ocean is within reach.

I always wanted a beach house
Since I was very young;
My family vacationed in summertime
At the coast for fun in the sun.

From Outer Banks of North Carolina
To the beach called Sagamore,
We'd spend two weeks of summer
Swimming and playing at the shore.
I have so many great memories
Of being near the sea.
The beach is my happy place
Where I love to be.

Truly I am a beach bum;
That's where I belong
Walking barefoot in the sand,
Singing to myself a song,

Feeling the misty breeze on my face,
Collecting stones and shells,
Watching for whales and dolphins,
Hearing stories the seagull tells,

Sitting under my umbrella
Reading a book, writing a poem,
Awaiting the beauty of sunset ~
The beach is my heart's home.

TERRY REDMAN

Shadows

shadows soften the glare of assertive colors,
the eye pauses to notice reality displayed
but missed in overexposure.

shadows caress the mind's eye.
imagination, fantasy, memory and yearning
paint in light and shadow in black/white.

shadows brings mystery and depth
to the game called developing.

FALL CONTEST WINNERS

On the Bus to Bethlehem

Ronald Jarrett (First Prize, 2017)

The wind races across the open plains of Oklahoma. It dares, taunts, teases, and arm-wrestles anything with the audacity to try and stand perpendicular to it. It playfully pushes silky white dunes of snow into every corner that, in weather like this, is silly enough to admit to being a corner.

My mother, my sister, and I wait for a bus. It is 1948; it is the season of Christmas, some would say the season of love, peace and brotherhood. Perhaps.

In a general store, cum bus station, we idle away our time. My mother, a college student on Christmas break, sits in a corner thumbing through a magazine, drinking coffee from a paper cup. She is twenty-four; her eyes reveal a wisdom beyond her time.

My sister talks. Her existence demands that she hear herself, but she has given up trying to talk to her mother. She decides to explain the truths of her six-year-old universe to the store owner. Perhaps he will respond.

I stand near a pot-bellied stove and ponder the whys of a five-year-old. Why does coal burn? Why does the burning coal heat up the stove? Why do pot-bellied stoves not heat up the corners of our lives? I walk to the window, watching the highway, but no bus. I'm apprehensive. I've never been on a bus before.

Looking has not helped my hopes, so I walk over and stand quietly by my mother, wondering what wonderful secrets are in the words she seems so intent on savoring.

My sister, seeing us together, assumes that a family meeting has been called and breaks off her monologue with the store owner. "Mother, if this bus doesn't hurry up, we could miss Santa Claus. He won't know where to find us. You know Santa always looks for us at Grandmother's."

It is clear to me that she has absolutely no knowledge of the ways of the universe.

Doesn't she know Santa is like God—incapable of error?

I move to the front of the store to look for the bus. It is just pulling in. "It's here," I shout, moving quickly to my mother. Even when girls are ready to go, it seems they are forever on the verge of missing the trip.

The three of us bundle up and exit the general store, the screen door slamming behind us, and climb aboard the bus. My mother moves with purpose to stake out the single seat in the back of the bus. I'm confused. The rear of the bus is crowded; the front of the bus is virtually empty. Why, I wonder, did we pass up rows and rows of empty seats?

My mother sits and puts my sister on her lap, giving her a pillow so she can sleep. Trying to be a man, I pretend to understand. But of all the people on the bus, I alone am standing. I feel different, an outsider, embarrassed. I want an explanation but I'm afraid to ask.

A man sitting behind the driver's seat spots me and walks to the back of the bus, speaking softly with my mother. I can't hear what is said, but my mother is smiling and nodding her head. The man turns to me and asks if I would like to sit with him. My mother smiles and assures me it will be alright. I take the man's hand and follow him to the very first row of the bus.

I'm more confused now than before, but the man is nice enough, even if he does talk funny.

The driver returns. As if by radar, he spots me and his face goes flush. Can he really be afraid of a five-year-old boy?

"I'm sorry son, but you can't sit here . . . you have to ride in the back with your kind."

I'm confused beyond hope, my eyes welling up with tears. The man puts his arm around me, squares his face to the driver and holds out his passport. In a voice loud enough for the entire bus to hear, he announces: "I beg your pardon sir, but this is my nephew. This child has just come with me to visit from the new State of Israel. This is the way people look in Israel." A hush prevailed over the bus, but the man was just beginning. "Surely, at this holy season, you are not about to deny a seat, a place of rest and comfort, to a weary traveler?"

"OK, Mac, OK, you made your point. . . and it being Christmas and all. . . ."

The Journey has begun. For me, it will never end. For the next two hours, the man fills my head with stories of a people and a time far removed. Stories of David, Moses, Solomon and Daniel. Stories of men, of action, of adventure, of overcoming adversity.

This bus ride, which began so strangely, will be all too short,

Tulsa, the destination, is the next stop. The skyline of the city looms like a small Manhattan. Its skyline has always been its pride. It would be years before I would discover its disgrace.

The bus stops and the man and I get off and wait for the two women. When they reach the front, my mother tries to thank the man. The man tries to thank my mother. It's a stand-off. The man smiles. She smiles.

The man speaks: "maybe someday." My mother, with a strength in her voice I've never registered before, replies: "No, my friend, not someday . . . very shortly!"

That evening, when she tucks me into bed, I'm full of a thousand questions about Mr. Katz.

"Mother, is Mr. Katz a Christian? He said he doesn't celebrate Christmas."

"That's because Mr. Katz is Jewish."

"Well, do you think the bus driver is a Christian?" "Probably, dear. Most people in this country are."

"Good, then when I grow up, I'm going to be Jewish."

"Ronald, I'm afraid it's not that simple. We are a Christian family."

"Why?"

"Why what?"

"Why are we a Christian family?"

"Because that's our religion."

"But I don't understand. Why would we want to be like the people who want little kids to stand up on bus rides and not like the people who care about little kids?"

"Ronald, what happened today had nothing to do with little kids; I've told you a dozen times. What happened to us today happened because we are a different color."

"But that's all the more reason I should become Jewish."

"Why would that be, pray tell?"

"Well, the way I see it, Mom, I can grow out of being a kid, but I can never grow out of my skin."

"Ronald, would you just go to sleep? The trouble with you, young man, is that you are always making your life difficult by asking questions . . . questions to which you are not old enough to know the answers."

I closed my eyes, pulled my dreams from behind my thoughts, and wondered if I would ever be old enough.

THE PORCH

Sue Jennings (Second Prize, 2017)

The old man rolled his walker to the back porch to watch the sun set like he and Nell had done for decades. But she'd passed and he now had only the remembrances of her. He fondled the paper cup she'd filled with a handful of soil and a seed for her vegetable garden before she said his name and slumped to the floor. He stared with moist eyes at the cross-stitch pillow of barn animals on her rocking chair. He shuffled to his rocking chair and plopped down. Buzzy laid his gray muzzle on his foot. He felt the breeze and heard pages of Nell's open Bible rustle on the table between their chairs.

Rubbing a scar on his arm, he remembered how in Korea he prayed for her letters, photos, and packages of cookies, candy, and boxes of sugary cereal to arrive. He smiled at the recall of how the guys in his squad swarmed around him like vultures at mail call. They knew he'd share his high school sweetheart's and mother's "care" packages. He did share the food and photos, but never shared her letters. They meant too much to him for a bunch of horny grunts to hear her devoted love for him.

He gently rocked, visualizing how she stood on this same porch stuffing a pillow the day he came home from Korea in 1953 and how his ma, stitching the end of striped ticking for another pillow, stood beside her. Pa, hands on his hips, stood with his back to him admiring the newly screened back porch. Pipe smoke swirled above his battered green John Deere cap. A hammer dangled from the loop on his overalls. The next day, against his doctor's caution to avoid aggravating his scarred skin and internal healing by stretching and lifting heavy items, he helped Pa hang the screen door.

They married three months later with the porch draped in red roses and white carnations as a back drop to the pastor pronouncing them in the eyes of God to be man and wife. He couldn't recall the date, but when the coroner asked how long they'd been married, he answered, "sixty-three years." When asked who should be contacted, he told the firemen and paramedics who'd responded to his frantic 911 call their first boy child arrived a year later. The boy was two when they were blessed with twin girls. He told them after a painful miscarriage, a year later a second boy was born. A little more organized in his thoughts, he later told the coroner he would contact his children.

To avoid him seeing his lifeless lover lifted on the gurney and covered with a sheet to be taken away from him through the open screen door, a fireman insisted he go to the kitchen. The same man blocked his view of the gurney going out the open screen door. He rambled knowing when he did look Nell would be gone. He pointed toward the porch mumbling how many times he'd repair the door after a dog Nell rescued burst through the screen to protect her garden from crows and black birds or chase a cat that dare enter their back yard.

Later, alone, the sun glowing on the other side of the world, the man stood on his arthritic knees to let Buzzy outside to do his business. Watching the dog sniff at the soil Nell had spaded for her spring planting, he was sad for the old mutt. He knew the dog would never understand why there would no longer be a garden to patrol or why the woman lay on the floor and despite pawing her hand she didn't pat his head and say, "You're my good boy."

He remembered coming home from work to find Nell bathing the ugliest flea-covered puppy she'd ever rescued in a tub of soapy water on the back porch. They'd been dogless for two months and he was getting used to the quiet and not having to take screen out of the tool shed to repair the door. But, like with all the dogs she'd taken in through the years, he loved her too much to say they didn't need a pet. Ten years later, Buzzy, his nose pressed against the screen, woofed and wagged his tail. Let inside, the man heard the clicking of nails on the hardwood floor as the bewildered dog searched the house for his friend.

Surrounded by darkness, he watched sheet lightning flash above the hills of the valley that'd been his home except for the two years he spent fighting for his country in Korea. A whisper of fear came with each flash and the rumble of thunder. He was always anxious with electrical storms. A similar lit sky in Korea wasn't the weather but a storm of artillery and mortar shells exploding over and around him. His face and chest buried in the snow, the ground trembling under his shivering, nineteen-year-old body, he prayed not to die. His prayers were partially answered when a shell detonated above his fox hole. Semi-conscious, feeling searing pain in his back and legs, and the smell of burning flesh, he knew he was alive.

Later, at the army hospital in Tokyo, he looked aghast where pebble-sized pieces of hot shrapnel had penetrated his skin leaving blood red scars. He worried how Nell would react to his maimed body. After six months in an army hospital he went home. Nell wasn't repulsed by the scars the first time he wore shorts and took off his tee-shirt, exposing his violated torso. The first time they made love she stroked the marred skin telling him the marks only made him more unique.

He dozed off and was startled when the grandfather clock in the hallway struck midnight. Nell's chair squeaked and began to rock. He hoped he was in a dream and would wake to Nell snoozing next to him. He slowly turned his head. Buzzy looked at him, whimpered and pawed the cross-stitch pillow, before turning twice, and then settled in Nell's chair. Tearfully, the old man accepted for the first time in over six decades he'd go to bed with the memory of his Nell in bed with him.

My Dad, My Hero

Gay Chambers (Third Prize, 2017)

Military life meant moving every year from one Army fort to another. This year, however, the destination was different. There were no forts in Wichita, Kansas, just Dad's brothers. Orders for Vietnam came through and Dad wanted us close to relatives just in case. At twelve years old, I didn't give the just-in-case scenario any thought. My father had already survived thirty-three missions flying a bomber over Germany, served a year in the Korean War, and spent 18 months in volatile Turkey—so I didn't think anything of this Vietnam deployment.

With lots of hugs, I said, "Goodbye." School started and our ordinary life resumed as we moved into our new home a block from my aunt and uncle. I had no clue how much our lives were about to change.

March 15, 1967, is a day burned into my memory. Mom was home alone when the doorbell rang. A taxi driver stood on the porch holding a telegram. With a quiet apology, he handed it to her and walked away.

I was at my aunt's when the phone rang. She answered, dropped the receiver, and tore out of the house, slamming the screen door behind her. A sense of dread welled up as I saw her turn toward my house. I ran after her.

When I entered the house, mom was lying down on the couch, pale and shaking. As I dropped to the floor next to her, she grabbed my hand.

My aunt explained, "Your dad's been wounded, but we don't know his condition because the telegram's over a day old." My heart raced as my stomach clenched with fear and everything after that was a blur.

My uncles burst through the door carrying a CB radio. They knew a HAM operator who might find someone with more information. After a few tense hours, they finally connected with the nurse overseeing Dad's care at Tan Son Knut Air Force Base in South Vietnam.

He was alive.

A few weeks later when Dad was stable, they transferred him to Fitzsimmons Hospital in Denver, Colorado and Mom flew out to be with him. During our phone conversations, the only thing Mom said was he looked different.

My sister and I were anxious to see him when we arrived in Denver. As we exited the hospital elevator, a frail, hunched over, withered man with a mask covering the lower part of his face stood waiting. But I recognized those piercing, blue eyes—they were my dad's eyes. I hugged him, but was afraid to squeeze too hard because he was so thin. His body trembled with fatigue after standing only a few short minutes. My dad was alive and in my mind, the doctors would heal him. Everything would be okay.

The next evening, mom hesitated outside his room and warned us that Dad wasn't wearing his mask. Then she opened the door.

There sat a monster.

A sniper's bullet had struck the back of his neck, ricocheted around his mouth and exited under his left eye. His face was flat, the bridge of his nose gone. One side of his misshapen jaws protruded further than the other one and a tube in his throat helped him breathe. Bile rose up into my throat and I felt sick.

My sister fell into Mom's arms sobbing, and I couldn't move. Then I looked into his eyes, the same eyes I'd seen yesterday, except now they were filled with sorrow. I took a deep breath, marched over to him, sat down in his lap, and laid my head on his shoulder. Tears slipped down his wounded face as he wrapped his thin arms around me.

It was a miracle that the bullet had missed his jugular vein, spinal cord, and brain. A fraction of an inch in any direction would have paralyzed or killed him.

His healing journey had just begun, but my life also changed.

Every day after school, I walked to the hospital, where helicopters methodically landed two at a time delivering more wounded. As I walked through the lobby, the x-ray department was on my left. Listless soldiers lay on gurneys lining both sides of the hall. Under each gurney, an additional soldier was lying on a stretcher. To my right, other G.I.s packed the waiting room of the prosthetics department. Some were waiting for measurements, while others received their new artificial limbs.

I continued to the elevator and punched the 4West button. The doctors didn't know where to place my dad, as he was an unusual case, so they put him with the amputees. The sight overwhelmed me every time I opened the door to the ward. Stretched out was row upon row of young men with missing limbs. Each day I had to walk past them to reach my father's room.

Because of the hole in the roof of Dad's mouth eating was a real problem. So the doctors made an incision in his stomach and pulled a section of the lining up for him to insert a feeding tube each time he needed sustenance. While he gently placed a rubber tube into his stomach, I would draw a protein concoction into a giant syringe then push the plunger to deliver his meal.

After each feeding, he'd smear petroleum jelly around the opening, then place several layers of gauze and tape over the top.

To keep stomach acid from leaking through the bandages, he had to recline in bed with only a pillow behind his head. Unable to do much in that position, boredom quickly set in. So my mother taught him to knit. I would spend the evenings by his bedside sipping soda out of a paper cup and doing homework, while he knitted sweaters for all our relatives.

One evening, he told me how he was wounded. "Bullets were pelting the dirt around me, so I turned and ran up the hill. When the bullet struck me, I spun around and landed on my back. A surreal peace surrounded me as I stared up at a clear blue sky and for the first time heard birds singing in the trees. I'm alive I thought, but when I tried to take a breath, I couldn't. I silently cried out to God asking why I had survived the bullet only to suffocate. Then I heard a voice saying, 'Roll over.' As I struggled to my side, something shifted and I began gulping the air. It's not something I like to think about too much, but, I'll never forget God's voice."

Three years later, after fifty reconstructive surgeries, Dad's face was as good as it would get. By this time, I was blind to the disfigurement. I see only Dad, my inspiration, mentor, and hero.

I'm forever grateful for the surgeons at Tan Son Knut Air Force base who wove together the splinters of Dad's lower jaw. The accomplishments of the plastic surgeons in the late 60's were amazing. None of the medical problems they foresaw in his future ever manifested.

Today he is 93 years old, active in church, and still knitting hats for missions in Peru.

MEMENTOS

Robert Kimsey (First Prize, 2016)

In the fall, when red maple leaves settle to carpet the forest floor and a cold wind rolls down the mountain, scattering them into a swirling trail of colors; when boots scuff hard against rocky ground and the last of the straggling deer pick their way through fallen branches toward the promise of sustenance in the south; that is when Sofi buries her mother.

She buries her in ground as hard and uncompromising as the old woman had been, listens as the priest says his words to an audience of one–for after ninety-eight years, Mother has outlived any potential mourners. She may not have had any regardless, nasty as she was to everyone, full of vinegar and bile, expelling a nice word more painful and protracted than giving birth. Sofi wants to be done with it–to be done with the memories of her childhood and the cold distant woman who had come as close as anyone to raising her.

After the funeral she goes back to her house, unchanged since she was a little girl except for the where the realtor has had people tearing dead brush from the front yard. The home is weathered and forlorn on its old plot. Mother lived there alone the last twelve years, ever since Sofi's father died. Few arrangements have been made, so it falls to Sofi to see to the place, to clean it out and get it ready for market because god knows Meg isn't going to leave her big city condo to do it. Sofi is left to clean, to deal with the real estate agent, and to take care of the boxes full of junk accumulated over the years, nothing thrown away because Mother lived through the depression and you didn't waste anything ever.

Sofi goes through the boxes one by one, like an archaeologist uncovering the layers of her childhood. She digs through the strata of outfits she and Meg once wore, perfectly preserved in plastic, a strange testament to some kind of sentiment in their harsh mother. She goes through the photo albums, curates them, takes out the pictures that mean most to her and lets the rest go because she doesn't have room for it all. The ones she saves are from when she and Meg are toddlers, when Mother still dresses them and does their hair, and the pictures show her smiling.

In one of the boxes, an old coffee pot. 1970s model Mr. Coffee, glass darkened by time and use, and Sofi remembers the soft gurgling that woke her every morning, the warm smell of whatever cheap tin can coffee her dad brought home. In Sofi's oldest memories, Mother is like that coffee pot–earthy, warm as long as you don't get too close, somewhat sterile both in terms of form and function. She has her purpose and she serves it faithfully, keeps the husband warm and happy, doesn't care to get outside of her sphere.

Or had she cared? Something changed as the girls grew older, the woman in the oldest pictures–the ones Sofi chose to keep–transforming into someone distant and sometimes mean.

Another box, this time a steel bird cage, former home of one cockatiel named Watson after Mother's beloved Sherlock Holmes stories. Sofi had hated that bird, hated the high whistle it never stopped making and the layers of newspaper she'd been forced to pull from the cage and replace with fresh sheets. Beneath the cage an old yearbook, class of 1950, and she thumbs through it, marveling at how much older everyone looked back then compared to her own yearbook pictures. She finds Mother, short black hair and matching cateye glasses, young and vibrant and as pretty as Dad always said, and beneath the photo the words "Most-Likely-to-SucceedGirl" in old typeface blurred around the edges.

But she hadn't succeeded, yearbook prognostications notwithstanding. At least, not in the way that text seemed to imply. She'd married and given birth and tended the home of a mechanic, raised two tomboys and tried to teach them culture and art but more often than not patched up skinned knees and pulled twigs from tangled hair.

Sofi's knuckles whiten around the bars of the cage as the image shifts her perspective. She sees the grueling piano lessons, the demands that she and Meg read, the slaps for failed homework, in a different light. This is her mother struggling within bars of suburban windows and doors, without even a whistle to let the outside world know she is there, her own hopes pushed and prodded and sometimes beaten into her little girls so that their most likely to succeed stories will come true. And when those stories don't take, and her girls prefer mud and sports to pianos and handsome clothes, this is her mother retreating to the innermost space of the birdcage, clinging to her perch and pressing her thin lips so she won't make a sound and no one will notice she is there.

The realization overwhelms, and Sofi leaves the house, wind stripping tears from the corners of her eyes. She leaves the boxes and memories before they pull her any farther into a childhood littered with bad memories.

Outside, red-cheeked from the wind and warming up the twenty-five year old Audi she will drive until it falls apart, Sofi sees the rose bush uprooted and left on the front lawn. There are no flowers, and the wood is dark against the ground. Still, she remembers Mother planting that bush, she and Meg helping dig the hole and holding the garden hose, but mostly just getting themselves wet and muddy and in the way. The bush was always brittle and cracked, and it never produced flowers, but Mother insisted on watering it. An irrational anger at the realtor flashes though Sofi, and she is seized with a wild urge to take the bush to the cemetery and plant it in the loose soil of Mother's grave. Maybe it will take root there.

The bush is old, yes, its branches dark and seemingly dead. Sofi presses her thumbnail along the length of a stem, finding dead wood after dead wood until finally her nail exposes green beneath. Plants can surprise you like that. They can be rough-edged and covered with thorns, beautiful at times but all sharp turns and hard edges at others. They sit, rooted in the soil, unable to seek better climes. But they live, and sometimes even prosper. And sometimes, if they blossom, they're really something to see.

Sofi wrangles the bush into the backseat of her car. The bush scrapes her. It sticks her with its thorns, punctures her upholstery. Sofi forgives it. It's a rose bush, after all. It doesn't know how to be anything else. It lays, skeletal, in the back seat as she drives.

It is crooked when she plants it, but it gives enough to the wind so as not to break, and something about its odd angles and tenuous grasp on the soil look quite at home in the new surroundings.

It's not an ideal location, but maybe a day will come when it blooms.

SIEMPRE BELLA: ALWAYS BEAUTIFUL

Joan Raymond (Second Prize, 2016)

Several sharp thwacks on the wood screen door roused Scott from a midday catnap. Normally he didn't rest, but after the early morning aerobics at Bench Press and a tap dance class the 81-year-old senior thought it might be best before fixing dinner. He grabbed his hat and glasses, "Coming, be there in just a minute."

He opened the door and shielded his eyes. The sun peeked under a thundercloud and reflected off the sidewalk blinding him for a split second. A casually-dressed woman in her thirties with shoulder length chestnut-brown hair, dark green eyes, and tiny, rust-colored freckles paced on his porch. She cleared her throat, "I'm trying to find a Scott Duarte. Does he still live here?"

He tipped his grey hat, "I'm Scott. And who might you be?"

"Helen Greggors. We've never met, but you know my mom." She clutched a small lavender envelope. "My mom is Madeline Fortney, but you probably remember her as Maddie Dunkirk…"

Scott extended his hand, "Nice to meet you Helen. You have your mother's eyes." He pointed inside, "Please come in. I'll make us some coffee. My ankle's telling me it's gonna rain soon."

As Scott pushed the switch on the coffee maker, Helen stood and cleared her throat again. She hesitated, "I… I have something for you from Mom. She wanted to make sure you got it before… before it was too late…" She thrust the letter into his hand. "I'm sorry, I must go. My contact information is on the envelope." She turned and dashed out the door as large raindrops began to dot the sidewalk again.

Scott stiffened. A flush of adrenaline rushed through his body. *Maddie Dunkirk? I haven't heard that name in fifteen years.* He closed the door and sat on the edge of his sofa. His hands trembled. He took a deep breath, slowly drawing in the scent from the paper. *Musk, Maddie's favorite.* He read the handwritten note:

My Dearest Scott,

Our years of friendship meant more to me than you'll ever know. No matter how I felt about myself you always made me believe I was beautiful. My days were brighter when we were together. My heart ached when you told me you couldn't settle down. I had to leave, but I never told you I loved you. Even after all these years, I've never forgotten or stopped loving you.

When I found out I was dying, I wanted to see you again and tell you this in person. But the cancer took over. I don't have the strength to keep fighting. After I'm gone will you fix my hair up special, like you did before? Will you make me beautiful one more time? Weave your fingers around my curls, let the ringlets fall on my face? Even though you never admitted it, I know we had something very special.

Your friend,

Maddie

Scott held the letter up to his chest. His eyes prickled remembering Maddie. *How she hooked her hand in my pocket as we walked. Freckles covering her nose and shoulders. Thick curly red hair tickling my cheek when we snuggled. Scent of Musk. Touches. Tingles. When she picked a white rose from her rose bush and ran it along my cheek, slow and sexy… I always blushed. She always giggled.*

"How could I let Maddie fade from my life? She's the first woman I really cared about since Adelaide. Maybe even loved…" Scott's thoughts drifted back through his past. A hairdresser for over forty years, he touched and held many women -- several of them after his work day was over. Maddie had seen the article in the newspaper, "Siempre Bella Celebrates 30 Years in Business" and couldn't resist the champagne celebration. They shared so much in common. Both of them born in January. Both grew up in Amarillo, five miles apart. Both moved to California in their twenties and eventually, both ended up in Los Angeles -- almost too much in common to be a happy coincidence. After retiring, he spent many days and nights with long-time clients who became close friends. Maddie quickly became one of his closest friends.

Fear of losing Maddie drove him away. Scott opened his wallet and removed a faded picture of a young woman. "Adelaide, you never knew I planned to ask you to marry me after that dance. I had the ring, the flowers. But ol' man Warren changed everything. Too drunk to drive; never even remembered hitting my car. After you died, I promised myself I'd never fall in love again. Kept my word, m' love. But now I wonder… did I do the right thing?"

Scott jumped up and rushed to his bedroom. He ransacked the top drawer of his nightstand, knocking over a tiny wire bird cage filled with a withered white rose. He dashed to the front room, grabbed his keys and the envelope and left. The steady rain slowed his trip to Memorial Hospital. He sprinted across the parking lot and stopped at the desk for directions.

The slender receptionist scanned her computer screen. "Friend or family?"

He stuttered, "Family, of course."

"Room 316. Elevator's around the corner. Check in with the charge nurse."

Scott's heart thumped in his ears. The elevator ascended… floor… by floor… by floor. He spotted an older nurse in the hall and between breaths managed to ask, "Maddie's room?" The nurse pointed to a large window across the hall.

Gripping the doorframe for support, Scott's eyes followed the tubes and wires snaking from Maddie's body. Machines beeped like metronomes keeping a steady tempo. Helen stood next to the bed, holding her mother's hand. She turned and whispered, "Thanks for coming." She stepped outside leaving them alone.

Scott's throat tightened, he fought back tears. "Maddie, Hun, it's me Scott. Can you hear me?" He caressed her frail hand. The freckles had faded; her grey hair thinned from chemo treatments.

She turned towards his voice and managed to whisper, "Scott." Her eyes glistened, "You shouldn't see me like this."

Scott smiled. "You look beautiful as always, Darling. I'm sorry we lost touch. I regret so much." Scott shared the story of Adelaide and the promise he made so many years ago. He caressed Maddie's neck and ran the back of his fingers along her cheekbone. Their eyes met and locked. "Hun, I should have asked you something years ago." He pulled a felt box from his pocket. His voice quivered. "Madeline, will you marry me?"

She smiled and nodded, too weak to talk. He held her hand and slid a small diamond ring on her thin finger, then bent over the bed rail and kissed her. She took a breath -- slow and deep, then closed her eyes. Scott buried his face in her silent chest and wept for the wasted years. He wound his finger around her thin curls and let a ringlet fall on her face. "You will be beautiful for your funeral My Love… always beautiful, siempre bella."

THE ONLY THING TO DO

Annis Cassells (Third Prize, 2016)

Robert raked his fingers through his lank salt-and-pepper hair. He pushed it back from his puffy eyes, stood and paced from the sofa to the window and back. Dr. Carter, his therapist, spoke, "She's not the mother you knew, Robert. Elva is a different person now. She doesn't even know who you are."

Robert flopped onto the brown leather sofa. Lifting his chin toward the ceiling, he said, "I know. I know." His voice, barely above a whisper, trailed off, and he went somewhere else, thinking about his last visit to Greenhall, the memory-care home where he'd placed his mom a month earlier. He'd taken her a butter-yellow Julia Child rosebush, a cutting from her yard, which he'd transplanted into a vibrant blue ceramic pot. Elva's face registered no recognition -- not of her favorite rose or of her son. For the third time in as many visits, he'd become discouraged.

"She won't miss you, Robert," Dr. Carter said. "And seeing her the way she is? Knowing she's lost to a different time and place and doesn't recognize you. How is that doing you any good?"

"She has no one else. I can't abandon her again," he said, his whiny adolescent voice reappearing. He stood again, crammed his fists into his jeans pockets, and paced. He patted his back pockets, located his cigarettes. "But the guilt. I don't think – I don't think I can deal with the guilt." He held up one hand like a policeman stopping traffic. "I have to go," he said, lighting a cigarette as he stepped over the threshhold.

Robert had stayed away most of his adult life, dropping out of community college to join the Navy. His desire to get away from his mother and the lure of faraway travel inspired that decision.

Elva'd kept him, her only child, close. She tried to stifle his curiosity about the world. Whatever he wanted to try, she'd say, "Oh,

Robby, that's too dangerous! You might get hurt. Then Mama would be so, so sad. Come, sit by Mama. I'll make us some popcorn. We can watch our shows and feed popcorn to Petey."

Petey, the African Grey parrot, was part of the family. When young Robby asked where Petey had come from, his mother held silence. Then, "He's always been with me. Always."

The bird's territory encompassed one whole corner of the living room. From his vantage point, in his square cage atop a large cherry wood table, Petey could see the television that played all day until bedtime. Because of this, and Elva's training, Petey possessed an extensive vocabulary. "Come on DOWN!" he'd squawk. Or he might repeat, "Days of our lives" while the popular soap opera played. Whenever Robert left the house, Petey's words echoed, "Bye, Robby! See ya' later!"

The morning Robert left for the Navy, his mother would not be consoled. Heartbroken, she refused to see him off. Robert stood outside her closed bedroom door and heard her rant, "I don't understand how he can abandon me, too! Just like his father."

He wondered what she meant, but finally, turned toward the front porch where the Navy recruiter stood waiting with Robert's duffle. "Well, so long," he whispered and walked away.

"Bye, Robby! See ya' later!" the African Grey sang.

During his 20 years in the Navy, Robert sent a few postcards home from foreign ports and visited his mother occasionally when on leave. After retirement, he lived and worked in Orange County. Each Christmas, he mailed a package to her, and once per summer, he visited. Though she tried to convince him to return home for good, he refused.

It was the phone call from Elva's neighbor that propelled Robert back to Bakersfield. "Robert, I hate to tell you this, but your mother is not well. She's not right. You better get home to see about her."

Elva had been pulled over by the police who had observed her veering to the side of the road, mounting the curb, then returning to the traffic lane. The police reported she was confused and unable to find her way home.

"She's at Memorial Hospital, son. We can go check on her, but you need to get home."

After a whirlwind drive up the Interstate and over the Grapevine, he arrived to take care of his mother's needs. "Mom. It's me," he said as he reached her hospital bed.

"Where have you been? Why were you gone so long? You shouldn't have left me, Peter. I was so worried about you."

"Peter? It's me, Mom. Robert. Your son."

"You got on that ship and sailed away. I still carry the picture that sailor snapped just before you went aboard."

"What are you talking about, Mom?"

"I still have our bird, Petey."

The more Robert tried to bring Elva to the present, the further away she went. Reminiscing about the days of her and Peter's young love. Deleting the past 48 years. Cherishing the memories of Peter. Telling an incredulous Robert everything she'd held back all his life.

Groggy from sleep, Robert staggered into the kitchen. He yawned and stretched, remembering his recent conversation with Dr. Carter. He groaned and mumbled, "That letter."

He pulled out a wooden bar stool, scuffing the feet across the splotchy linoleum. Perched on one hip, he reached for his pack of Camels and lighter on the tile counter. He picked up the coffee pot and poured yesterday's brew into yesterday's stained mug. He placed it in the microwave and pressed Start. *Six months,* he thought. *I've been doing this for six months.* He paced in front of the counter and several times removed the cigarette from his dry lips, eyed it a moment, then replaced it.

Robert tugged on the door of the microwave, reached in and extracted the thick, hot coffee. He scooped up his lighter and cell phone then stopped at the kitchen desk, grabbed the pad of onionskin airmail paper, an envelope, and pen. Sliding the patio door open with his elbow, he stepped out barefooted onto the cool cement. At the glass-topped table, he stopped, set everything down, and dragged out a wrought-iron chair. He dropped onto the cushioned seat, flicked open his lighter and was soon inhaling and holding the smoke inside his chest until the smoke rolled from his lips in perfect circles.

"I'd better get to it," he said aloud, rubbing the fingers of his left hand back and forth above his eyebrows. He picked up the pen and wrote:

My Darling Elva,

We've had some close calls, but I am safe. I miss you and can't wait for this miserable war to be over. Then I can hold you in my arms again. We had so little time together.

Robert was into the second paragraph when the ring tone he'd set for Greenhall Gardens sounded. "Yes?" he answered, his heartbeat on hold.

"Mr. Robert Stinson? Son of Elva Stinson?"

"This is he," he said, choking around the lump in his throat.

"Greenhall Gardens calling," the kindly voice said. An eternity passed. "Your mother is asking for you."

"For, for me?"

"Yes. She said, 'I want to see my Robby boy.'"

The Tunnel of Love

Richard Meeks (First Prize, 2015)

When Henry Gilmore read in the Sunday paper that the Fowler Brothers Carnival was closing, he knew he had to visit his and Maddie's favorite haunt one more time.

At eighty-five plus, his palsied hands and ailing ticker made once manageable tasks difficult, but he could still drive a car.

Henry's daughter, Nancy, with whom he lived, was aghast when he told her his plan.

"A man in your condition has no business wandering around a dusty carnival. Why bother all those roustabouts who are tearing it down? I'll bet they won't allow you to get near the place."

He shrugged. "It's on my bucket list of things to do—while I'm still above ground."

The next afternoon, perambulating along the carnival midway, he accepted his daughter's evaluation of his health. Pain permeated his spine, his legs ached, and his chest throbbed. Rivulets of sweat fogged his spectacles as he searched for the special spot.

The Tunnel of Love sign at last came into view, and he breathed a sigh of relief. "There it is, just as I re… what the hell?— SOMEBODY PULLED THE PLUG!"

He stepped closer and saw there was no longer a ticket booth in front of the ride. Also missing were the rowboats and the water. A damp, hollow shell was all that remained of the attraction so popular with lovers.

When sure no one was watching, he waddled over and peered into the tunnel's high arched entrance. Shallow standing pools here and there gave testimony that the ride had indeed been drained.

The dim, hollow interior called to him, and he began a slow, shuffling movement along the tunnel's walls. Thick, damp air made breathing difficult, aggravating the squeeze in his chest. Farther in, the lack of illumination made him wish he'd thought to bring a flashlight. For half its length, the tunnel traveled a direct path, then curved, before straightening again to exit into a wooded glen, with a large oak tree at its center.

Henry took off his glasses and stuck them in his shirt pocket; they were useless in this dark labyrinth. He rubbed his eyes, straining to remember how he felt sixty years ago when the young Henry Gilmore first accompanied his sweetheart, Maddie, through this same tunnel of love.

The bass drum in his chest pounded a fortissimo beat as grainy images from an unfocused camera danced before him. Now the focus sharpened, revealing a young couple in a rowboat moving along a stream of water. Overhead, embedded lights became twinkling tiny stars, keeping time to the soulful Phil Phillips tune, *Sea of Love*, wafting through the tunnel's speakers.

Henry and Maddie had been dating for a year. His heart had pounded then, too, because he'd planned for weeks to use this occasion to ask her to marry him.

When they reached the curve of the tunnel, he stopped rowing and searched in his pocket for the ring. Taking her hand in his, he gazed into her blue eyes.

"All right, Maddie, marry me or I'll make you walk the plank."

She giggled, trembling as Henry fumbled with the ring. When he attempted to slide it on her finger, it slipped out of his hand and bounced off the side of the boat.

"Oh, Dear… NO!" Maddie pulled off her shoes and stepped into the knee-deep water. Henry joined her, and the two searched the tube's murky bottom for this symbol of his devotion.

The dark curve of the tunnel and the inky water made it impossible to locate the ring, and they finally gave up the search. Drenched, they got back in the boat and rowed to the ride's exit. It was but a few steps to the big oak tree where they sat to dry out.

Henry put his arms around the shivering Maddie, who was near tears. "I'm sorry, Dear, for being so nervous. I guess we'll never find the ring."

"Don't think twice about that. I had the thing insured." He grinned. "Besides, you haven't earned it yet. You never answered my question."

"The answer is yes… OH, YES! Even though I think you made me walk the plank before I could give you my reply."

They sat in the warm sun, holding hands, swearing their lifetime allegiance. After a while, Henry stood up and took out his pocket knife. At the base of the big tree, he carved the words, *To Maddie, with love as solid as this oak. Henry. May 1955.*

That allegiance did last a lifetime, ending only with Maddie's death from breast cancer two years earlier. Without her, Henry struggled to carry on. She had been his soul mate, his reason for being. Their home held too many memories, so he sold it and moved in with his daughter. Most days he spent revisiting his and Maddie's favorite haunts, hoping they would help bring her closer to him in spirit.

So, when Henry read in the paper that the carnival was closing, he knew that he had to visit their special spot one more time. Now, as he labored through the drained tunnel, the memories overwhelmed him.

With each step, his chest pain intensified. When he reached the point where the tunnel curved, he squatted on its damp surface to rest. The light was better here, and he sat, calculating the amount of energy required to make it to the exit.

As he stood again, his eye caught a glint of something wedged in a crack in the concrete floor. Though covered with grime, the tiny object sparkled. He used his handkerchief to extract it from its hiding place and saw it was a ring. There was writing on the band, and he fumbled for his glasses. The inscription read: *To Maddie, with my undying love. Henry—May 1955.*

His failed attempt to place the engagement ring on Maddie's finger, that painful memory from half a century past, came rushing back to him.

Images swirled and danced as the tunnel's dim glow began to fade. Strange shapes tripped the light fantastic before his eyes, moving in rhythm to the song reverberating in his head.

Come with me, to the sea,

Come with me to the sea of love.

I wanna tell you, just, how much I love you,

I wanna tell you, oh, how much I love you…

Henry wiped away tears as the shapes gradually metamorphosed into the shimmering outline of a young woman. Now Maddie was there, looking radiant. She leaned close to him, pointed to the ring, and whispered, "Is that for me, Dear?"

He kissed her hand, slid the ring on her left index finger and said, "Honey, I've waited sixty years for this second chance."

Maddie helped her husband to his feet, and as they embraced, Henry exhaled a long, peaceful sigh. Then, arm in arm, the couple exited *The Tunnel of Love* one last time, heading for the big oak tree where he had perpetuated their love so long ago.

Going Home

Annis Cassells (Second Prize, 2015)

I stood on the platform at Gate 14 with a hundred other people, craning our necks, standing on our toes, searching the rails for the incoming train. It was late. The marquee's bright yellow digital letters flashed the train's destination and the delayed arrival time. But we all kept alert, some of us anxious to board, others eager to see their loved ones and hug them up as they disembarked.

My sister had phoned. "You'd better come now," she said. "I told Mom you were coming. She's waiting. For you."

"I'm on my way," I said, eyeing the project I'd been commissioned to complete by the end of this month. "I'll be there as quick as I can." I checked my watch. Ten a.m. I could catch the Amtrak San Joaquin, leaving Jack London Square at 1:15 and arrive in Bakersfield before dark. I caromed between my bedroom and my desk, stuffing my red carry-on and putting work papers into my brown leather briefcase. I had time to make a couple of quick Skype calls.

It wasn't until the hot shower water blasted the top of my head that I allowed myself to cry, to bellow, to scream. To curse about the unfairness of it all. To feel the pain of not being a dutiful daughter.

Mom's illness had surfaced two months before when she didn't feel "right" and went to her doctor. A CT scan, blood tests, and a PET scan showed stage four liver cancer. The news shocked and shook the family, my sis in Bakersfield and our brother in Colorado. Sure, Mom was eighty; but she'd always been strong and healthy, our rock.

The train whistle howled in the distance and movement commenced on the platform. A garbled announcement floated from the loudspeaker, sending a few wayward greeters back behind the yellow line.

I boarded the train and found a seat away from the passengers who had remained aboard. Then, I texted my sis, "I'm finally on the train. Fifteen minutes behind schedule. I'll keep you posted re: arrival time."

Before we could pull away from the station, my car filled up. An older woman dressed in a navy blue pants suit and a matching fedora atop her loose, gray hair wriggled into the seat beside me. I acknowledged her and scooted over a couple of inches then swept my eyes back toward the window.

"Well, young lady, are you going all the way to Bakersfield? That's where I'm heading. To see my daughter. I think you must be about her age. Are you visiting or going home?"

"Home," I mumbled and closed my eyes. "Going. Home."

"Oh, my. Is something wrong at home?"

"Everything. Everything is wrong." I told her. "I'm going home to see my mother for the last time. She's dying." I turned away, groping for a tissue in my purse. The partially used Kleenex wasn't up to the task and was soon in shreds as tears slid down my cheeks.

My chatty seat mate had turned silent. She held out an embroidered white hanky and motioned toward me, urging me to take it. "Honey, I am so sorry," she said as I unfolded the hanky and mopped my face. She placed her warm brown hand over mine and held it there. I didn't move. Her warmth felt good on my cold, trembling hands.

"Tell me about it," she said, peeking from beneath her hat brim, her posture, eyes, and touch inviting me to tell my story.

She never moved her hand from mine as the train swayed and its wheels clickety-clacked southward. I told her about Mom's illness, how I'd allowed my job to consume me and had only gone down to see Mom once or twice since her diagnosis. And about my sister calling this morning, saying Mom was waiting for me.

Waiting for me to arrive before she will die, I thought. Aloud, I said, "If I don't get there, maybe she won't die."

"You know it doesn't work like that," the sweet-faced woman holding my hand said. "But her will power won't let her slip away before tomorrow." I fumbled and found a dry spot on her hanky and dabbed my eyes again.

"I hope so."

"Now, what do you want to tell her? What last words do you want her to take with her when she passes through that golden tunnel, the pathway into heaven's light? Pretend I'm her. Tell me."

And I did. All the way down the San Joaquin Valley, between station after station, flowed 25 years' worth of memories, an outpouring of love and gratitude, and plenty of regrets and apologies. Somewhere around Visalia, exhausted, I laid my head on the woman's soft navy blue encased shoulder and dozed.

When the train came to an abrupt stop in Bakersfield, my eyes snapped open. I stretched and turned to speak to the kind woman. Her spot was empty except for a fresh, clean white hanky. I picked it up then searched up and down the aisle among the eager crowd waiting to exit the train. Peering out the dirty window, I noticed a blue hat float out of the crowd and, soon, saw her enveloped in a younger woman's arms. *Her daughter,* I thought. *I never even asked her daughter's name -- nor hers.*

"I'm here!" I texted my sister.

The message came back, "Me, too!" Excitement rose in my stomach like a swarm of bees.

Most of the travelers had descended from the train car before I stood to retrieve my bag and brief case from the overhead rack. I approached the doorway and gazed on my sister's face -- for the moment, she seemed carefree, just picking up her baby sis after a journey.

We stood on the platform and hugged a good long time, a silent hug that shouted with emotion. I felt myself stand erect, growing taller in the moment. Sis picked up my bag and, arms draped over each other's shoulders, we headed toward the parking lot. "How's Mom?"

"Waiting."

"Good. I have a lot to tell her. Let's go home."

CUB

Louis Medina (Third Prize, 2015)

"Ay!" Adriana stumbled. Her heel had caught in a crack on the cement floor of the tunnel, whose walls amplified the rattling of the glasses and plates inside the fancy picnic basket she was carrying.

"Cuidado! Careful!" Jose said in Spanish, as Adriana grabbed his arm for support. When she didn't let go once they continued walking, he looked down at her girly nails, newly done in glittering red polish.

"You shouldn't have worn those shoes."

"I wanted to look nice for you."

"You can do that without looking all hoochie," he scolded, eyeing her up and down. "Honestly: a tight pink dress and red stilettos to go on a picnic by the river."

"I've told you--"

"Yes, 'It's my style,'" he mocked her. "But look at how you clash with my sneakers, jeans and T-shirt. And how are you going to get down the riverbank?"

"I'll take off my shoes...And you'll help me." She kissed him on the cheek, making him smile.

This gesture—like her taking his arm—felt strange for both of them.

They were almost at the end of the pedestrian tunnel underneath the railroad tracks. There was the old dead tree on the other side, overgrown with crawling vines that had killed it, then dried up and died themselves.

"Our totem tree is still there," Jose told her.

"Like the tree near that other tunnel," she said, referring to the culvert between Mexicali and Calexico that Jose had crawled through to come to the United States a decade before, looking for something better for himself and his family. The same one she had come across five years later when he'd paid a *coyote* to bring her to him.

They had prayed together at that other tree, grateful for Adriana's safe passage.

When she was still Jose's son.

§

"Adrian, hijo! Que te han hecho?! What have they done to you, Son?!"

Adrian's face when he arrived was still bruised and swollen from the last beating he'd taken at school in Guatemala. His ribs were sore and it hurt to breathe. He winced when his father hugged him tightly.

"Aqui no queremos maricones! We don't want faggots here!" his classmates had screamed as they beat him to the ground and kicked him mercilessly.

His mother, Ana, didn't want the 16 year-old at home, either. Too much trouble having *"un hijo afeminado,"* she told Jose on the phone while Adrian listened. She feared he might be a bad influence on his younger brothers, Fernando and Gabriel, she said.

Jose didn't think twice about bringing him to be with him. He loved all his children but Adrian was the eldest, the first fruit of his loins. He had vowed to love the baby unconditionally—and to protect it—as soon as he'd found out Ana was pregnant and before he even knew whether he would have a son or a daughter. Or both.

He would finish raising Adrian in the U.S. while continuing to send money home to Ana and his other boys. There was more tolerance here: laws to shield his "effeminate son" from constant bullying. Maybe Adrian could even qualify for amnesty on the grounds of protection from persecution for his sexual orientation in his native country.

What Jose hadn't expected, however, was Adrian's tearful plea after he finished high school: *"Papi,* I've never really felt like a boy. I'm tired. I want to live as a girl." The revelation had come three years ago, the last time they'd crossed the tunnel under the tracks to go fishing, a pastime Jose enjoyed but Adrian did not. Neither of them had gotten a nibble that day. They walked home weighted down with uncertainty and anxiety.

In the months that followed, Jose had come back often to fish and think alone, each time stopping at the totem tree to say a prayer: "Please, I just want my son to be happy. Give me the wisdom to help him."

The answer came as he and Adrian were sitting on the couch one day watching a nature documentary about hyenas, that most vilified species of scavengers and pack hunters that Jose had somehow always liked. There was something about their laugh, their cunning, their strange appearance—not quite feline, not quite canine. What he learned about them this time, though, with great fascination, was that the females have an extended clitoris that looks uncannily like a male organ through which they mate and give birth.

"You see," Adrian said, "nature itself celebrates sexual diversity. It's only people who are all hung up with their prejudices and taboos."

Jose listened without taking his eyes off the television screen. He spoke only after his voice caught up with his conscience: "If you want me to go with you to counseling before you start the hormone treatment, I'll be there."

Adrian hugged his father, then lay with his head on Jose's lap for the rest of the show, just as he had liked to do as a child.

Witnessing the change from Adrian to Adriana was strange for Jose: the loss of facial hair and the heightened pitch of Adrian's voice; a whole new wardrobe, especially following the growth of breasts that Adriana augmented with implants; the frequent tears that flowed easily, he thought, because of all the estrogen Adriana was taking.

She, however, knew her tears were torrents of love and gratitude for her father's acceptance.

§

They were on the other side of the tunnel now, the totem tree before them, the river on the other side of a berm beyond.

Adriana stopped. Her transformation was finished. She had told her father the night before that she wouldn't be having genital reassignment surgery and invited him on today's picnic to celebrate. But there was something she still needed to know. She put down the picnic basket.

"Papi…"

"What is it?"

"Are you disappointed in me? Do you have any regrets about being my father?"

Jose looked at Adriana, placed his hands on either side of her face, and leaned her downward so he could reach her forehead for a kiss.

"A daughter shouldn't be taller than her father," he said. "You are. And with those high heels you insist on wearing, you tower over me like a giantess."

Adriana clung onto her father like a vine. The sobs, torrents of love, came gushing over her again, pure, loud and unstoppable.

Jose still wasn't used to having Adrian's—Adriana's—breasts press up against him when they hugged.

Embarrassed, he looked toward the totem tree. For an instant, he thought he saw the comical face of a hyena with slightly rounded ears and dark, mask-like markings looking at him from underneath the tangle of dry vines encasing the dead tree trunk. But he blinked and his magical totem animal, a vision—but one that had birthed hope in him, nonetheless—was gone. What was real and remained was what he held in his arms: his son, his daughter, his cub, pressed up against his chest like the wailing newborn he had held for the first time in fatherly love and protection, in what now seemed like two lifetimes ago.

CONTRIBUTORS

Authors

Anke Hodenpijl
Anke Hodenpijl spends much of her time contemplating nature, connecting with friends, traveling, singing at the bedside and writing poetry. She talks of deep things to her three dogs and partner, Judy. She relishes their responses. She's found that words are important, yet sometimes unnecessary. Laughter is always necessary.

Annis Cassells
Annis Cassells is a writer, poet, life coach, and teacher. She divides her time between Bakersfield, California, and Coos Bay, Oregon. Her poetry has been published in Yellow Chair Review, Scarlet Leaf Review and ITWOW 6th Anthology, and the California State University, Bakersfield's Community Poetry Anthology, 2016 and 2017. She has been a member of Writers of Kern for more than a dozen years.

Brent Gill
Brent was born in southeastern Tulare Country in 1944, raised on a ranch, married a city girl in 1965, and lives in the foothills. They have three married sons, eight grandkids, two dogs, two horses, eight cows, and a kissing bull. He writes a weekly column for the Porterville Recorder.

Carla Martin
Carla is a substitute teacher by morning, a poet in the afternoon and a pianist in the evening. She enjoys creating feasts for the eye, the stomach and the soul. Life has blessed her with the roles of mother, lover and critique group partner. She is very grateful.

Gay Chambers
Gay Chambers helped young readers discover the joy of reading as a school librarian. Now retired, she is currently working on a children's series for young readers. Gay serves on the Sunshine Committee of Writers of Kern, is an avid quilter, and heads up a baby care ministry.

Janet Skibinski
Originally from Cincinnati, Janet now calls Bakersfield her home. Her love of writing began in elementary school and has continued throughout her life. Published in a collection of stories about kindness, she's had articles in *The Bakersfield Californian.* She wrote a monthly newsletter for Quota International of Bakersfield.

Joan Raymond
Joan holds a B.A. and M.A. in Creative Writing/English. She is a professional writer and editor and teaches creative writing classes. In her spare time, she enjoys reading cozy mysteries and designs handmade cards and journals. She lives in Bakersfield with her family.

Judy Kukuruza
Judy Kukuruza is a retired college instructor and author of the memoir, *One Body Many Souls.* Living with her devoted and beloved pet, Sara, Judy blogs and writes daily while working to make ends meet. She writes because she believes every voice counts and should be heard.

Julie Bonderov
Julie is a voracious reader who enjoys children, animals, music and color. She is an RN who worked in local hospitals in pediatrics and now works with children as a school nurse. She enjoys encountering other cultures, languages and cuisine. Julie collects how to say, "Don't cry," in other languages.

LaVerne Lovelady
LaVerne Lovelady is a retired teacher of English. She began a love-affair with classic Interpretive Literature at age twelve, when a neighborhood librarian introduced her to William Shakespeare. She paid the experience forward by facilitating a high school poets' club, from which several unique poets emerged and continue to write & publish.

Lois Henry
Lois Henry grew up on a ranch east of Fresno and attended Fresno State. She moved to Bakersfield in 1990 and spent nearly 30 years working as a journalist. But she started out wanting to write fiction.

Louis Medina
Born in El Salvador. Raised in the U.S. Spent 1.5 decades of his adult life in Japan, Spain, and England. Wrote for *The Bakersfield Californian* from 2006-

2009 and has worked for nonprofits—his calling—since. Louis Medina's writing is informed by the world—of humans and animals.

Mandy Wallace
Mandy Wallace—business writer at Hypist.com, founder of Write or Die at mandywallace.com, spends more time avoiding writing than she actually writes.

Nelson Varon
A poet and former professional musician, school teacher, piano and organ retailer, board member of a publicly traded corporation, magazine publisher, shopping center developer, a published songwriter and a published author of several music instruction methods. Nelson Varon is proud to be an Active member of WOK.

Pam Reeves
Recently retired from the corporate world where she wrote professionally and technically, Pam Reeves is a late-blooming independent writer. She's a member of the Writers of Kern in Bakersfield, California, and writes memoir, non-fiction, blogs and even tries her hand at a little poetry from time to time.

Portia Choi
Portia Choi promotes poetry hosting First Friday Open Mic and publicizing National Poetry Month in April. She administers www.kernpoetry.com. She is in the poetry critique group of Writers of Kern. She published a poetry chapbook *Sungsook, Korean War Poems.* Her email is portia@kernpoetry.com.

Richard Meeks
Richard Meeks taught middle school instrumental music with the Bakersfield City School District for thirty-six years. Since his retirement, he has been pursuing his passion for writing fiction. He has been a member of the Writers of Kern for the past fifteen years and hopes to one day finish his novel in progress.

Robbie Byrne
Robbie Byrne is the recipient of the BBC Playwright of the Year award; has had various theater dramas performed in the UK; six novels published since 2002, and is excited about his work appearing in the WOK anthology. He is married and resides in Bakersfield, California.

Robert Kimsey
Robert is a writer, editor, and intellectual property attorney. He has published short stories, a children's book, and edited anthologies and e-zines. When not engaged in one of these pursuits, he caters to the whims of his cat, Molly.

Ronald Jarrett
Ronald grew up in Tulsa, Oklahoma. He went to the University of Maryland, Eastern Shore, then joined the Air Force. He went to law school at Colombia University. He's a lawyer, a college professor (Florida A&M) and a writer. He's retired and living in Bakersfield, California with his wife Martha.

Rose Wilstead
Rose was born and raised in Bakersfield, California. She attended Quailwood Elementary School. An aspiring author, she writes children's and fantasy stories. Learn more at www.kindgirlsmakestrongwomen.com.

Shelley Evans
Named after the poet Percy Bysshe Shelley, nature inspired Shelley Evans to write poetry as a young girl. Several of her poems have been published, and she is preparing her first book for publication. Shelley is a legal secretary, wife, mother, Active member of WOK. She attends open mic nights.

Sue Jennings
Born and raised in Bakersfield, Sue attended local high schools and Bakersfield College. before attending Cal-Poly San Luis Obispo. Earning a bachelor's degree, Sue worked as a Child Protective Services social worker, supervisor, and administrator until retirement. Sue remembers writing VERY BAD stories in the third grade.

Terry Redman
Terry's card says, "Mystery Fan, Bibliophile, Writer, Raconteur." He has been published in non-fiction, fiction and poetry genres. Writing fiction is fun, but he does it poorly. Self-publishing projects produced a book about coffee houses and two books about his family tree. Reading includes suspense and biography. Creative blank verse is his current passion.

Photographer

Lori Lovelady

Lori Lovelady is best known for her canvas paintings, graphic arts and crisply focused photographs. As a means of dealing with family tragedies, Lori turned to photography as well as authored and illustrated the children's book, *Nattie's Daddy*, dedicated to her son Nathanael, who was tragically killed in a car accident.